Training Soprano Voices

Training Soprano Voices

Richard Miller

OXFORD
UNIVERSITY PRESS

2000

OXFORD
UNIVERSITY PRESS

Oxford   New York

Athens   Auckland   Bangkok   Bogotá   Buenos Aires   Calcutta
Cape Town   Chennai   Dar es Salaam   Delhi   Florence   Hong Kong   Istanbul
Karachi   Kuala Lumpur   Madrid   Melbourne   Mexico City   Mumbai
Nairobi   Paris   São Paulo   Singapore   Taipei   Tokyo   Toronto   Warsaw

and associated companies in
Berlin   Ibadan

Copyright © 2000 by Oxford University Press

Published by Oxford University Press, Inc.
198 Madison Avenue, New York, New York 10016

Library of Congress Cataloging-in-Publication Data
Miller, Richard, 1926–
Training soprano voices / Richard Miller.
p.   cm.
Includes bibliographical references and index.
ISBN 0-19-513018-9
1. Singing—Instruction and study.   2. Sopranos (Singers)—
Training of.   I. Title.
MT820.M5995 2000
783.6'6143—dc21   99-27828

7 9 8 6

Printed in the United States of America
on acid-free paper

Honoring the memory of Ruth Cogan,
who inspired so many

Acknowledgments

I want to express my thanks to Maribeth Anderson Payne, Executive Editor, Music, Oxford University Press, for her encouragement regarding the conception of this book, to Robert Milks for his cheerful assistance during the production process, to Anton Mattias Miller for his help in the preparation of music examples, and above all to Mary Norman Miller for her judgment, discernment, caring, and invaluable help in all aspects of my daily work.

Contents

Training Soprano Voices

Introduction

TEACHERS OF SINGING OFTEN CONFESS THAT IT IS EASIEST TO IN-
struct a student of one's own voice type. There are more sopranos than singers of all
other voice categories combined. Inasmuch as most singing teachers are themselves
sopranos, it might be presumed there is little need for a special volume devoted to
the training of soprano voices. Further, it would seem that principles of good voice
production apply to all voices. Sopranos, together with contraltos, mezzo-sopranos,
tenors, baritones, bass-baritones, and basses, are subject to laws of physiology and
acoustics equally applicable to all singers. Why then a separate volume on training
soprano voices?

Universal measures apply to each soprano voice, but the diversity of instruments
within the general soprano category requires variations in pedagogic application. A
young dramatic soprano voice must not be forced into a soubrette mold, nor ought
the soubrette soprano be assigned dramatic tasks. Subtle differences in categories
of the soprano voice are based on variations in physiognomy, laryngeal size, shape of
the resonator tract, points in the musical scale where register events occur, and personal imaging. The plan of this book is to identify subdivisions within the general
designation of "soprano" and to offer suggestions and practical vocalises appropriate for the several types.

Functions of the tripartite instrument are examined:

1. motor activity (mechanical aspects of breath application in singing),
2. vibratory response (laryngeal response to airflow during singing), and
3. resonance factors (vocal tract filtering and language articulation, and their
   effect on the complex vocal sound).

Practical technical exercises to achieve functional unification of this tripartite instrument are introduced. These systematic exercises are supplemented by vocalization
material taken from the performance literatures of the soprano categories.

Categories of the Female Voice

Zerlina and Brünnhilde, according to the designations given them by Mozart and Wagner, are both sopranos. Having Brünnhilde sing "*Batti, batti*" would parallel entering a diesel-powered transport van in the classic Indianapolis 500. Zerlina cannot be put astride Grane for an *Immolation Scene* excursion without being headed for vocal incineration. Brünnhilde and Zerlina are separated from each other by a wide gulf of laryngeal and vocal-tract construction. From contralto to soubrette/coloratura, the category (*Fach*) of each female voice is largely determined by the physiology of the instrument itself, the location of voice-register demarcations, and adherence to specific tonal concepts.

Although some few artists of the past were far ranging as operatic protagonists (though surely not so diverse as Zerlina and Brünnhilde!), no soprano can be expected to successfully take on roles that go beyond her natural endowment. Just as a *tenore di grazia* is not counted on to sing Siegmund or a *Heldentenor* to assay Almaviva, so must the diverse literature requirements of distinct soprano subcategories be kept clearly in mind. Even the most stable vocal technique does not permit a singer to undertake all facets of the repertoire.

Three traditional female vocal types are commonly specified: soprano (extensive), mezzo-soprano (less frequent), and contralto (rare). These broad classifications fail to detail the wide spectrum of characteristics among individual female voices. Females no more sound alike in speech and song than they look alike. How to tailor training procedures for dissimilar soprano categories is a matter of concern for both the singer and the teacher of singing.

The vocal instrument is not solely the larynx; it consists of the whole body. Just as gender, physiology, metabolism, and psychological orientation determine variations in human behavior, so do they in the production of the singing voice. An awareness of both the commonality of function and the individuality of each soprano voice must be constantly kept in mind.

An important aspect of voice training is to recognize what are reasonable expectations at appropriate developmental stages for each category. The potential dramatic soprano should not be expected to accomplish tasks suited to her soubrette counterpart of the same chronological age. Conversely, although many measures are applicable to all sopranos, it ought not to be assumed that a young soprano should be able to tackle dramatic literature if only she will sing it "lightly." The tessitura of the role, the density of the orchestral writing, and the intensity of the drama all belie the notion that singing dramatic literature at a low dynamic level makes it an acceptable assignment for a lightweight singer. Soprano voices of dissimilar size are not meant to attempt identical maneuvers at comparable periods of technical development.

Early in any discussion of soprano categories and how to adapt instruction for each, some mention should be made of a prevalent assumption that music for the high female voice written before the verismo movement of the late nineteenth century is reserved to the light soprano. As has been the case in the development of musical composition over the past four centuries (itself a study in evolving voice categorization), composers' demands have increased in accordance with mounting recognition of the technical potentials of the human vocal instrument. (Evolution of the literature for voice is paralleled in instrumental writing—witness the keyboard, wind, and string-instrument literatures.) As the most enduring works illustrate, skillful composers early began to take into account the weight and range of the solo vocal instrument. Regardless of voice category, the compositional trend was to write for singers who could compete with increasing instrumental volume and with the acoustic demands of expanded performance spaces. Music of the eighteenth century and of the bel canto period should not be restricted to the soprano voice of small dimension.

It should be added that sizable performance spaces were not a late-nineteenth-century development. Large performance rooms and theaters were not unusual even during the seventeenth century; the great halls of many *palazzi* where Baroque opera was regularly presented could accommodate several thousand listeners. The professional vocalist was already in ascendance in the late works of Monteverdi.

Small performance rooms were not as typical of the eighteenth century as is often supposed. Fux's *Costanza e fortezza* was performed in Prague in 1723 on an open-air stage that had a depth of over 220 feet.[1] The Grande Salle at the Palais Royal, built in 1770, housed an audience of over 2,000.[2] King's Theatre in the Haymarket, London, built in 1782, seated 1,800 persons; the new London theater constructed in 1793 could serve 3,300 spectators.[3] It cannot be assumed that until the second half of the nineteenth century most public performance took the form of salon art.

In four hundred years, the singing instrument itself has not undergone significant physical change. Truly historically informed performance cannot ignore these enduring physiologic factors. In view of the extended vocal demands found in the works of Haydn, Mozart, Beethoven, Bellini, Donizetti, and Rossini, it cannot be maintained that noted performers in the latter part of the eighteenth century and the first half of the nineteenth century were vocal miniaturists. In addition, good voice function and beauty of timbre were among the universal aims of the historic teachers of singing. These objectives should continue to undergird all voice instruction.

In the search for beautiful and healthful singing, the singer or teacher does not need to invent a unique system of voice pedagogy. All technical maneuvers can be codified into existing methodologies. Some are more efficient than others. A goal of this book is to determine how effective function (vocal freedom) can best be achieved.

Are there basic techniques of singing applicable to all voices, soubrette through basso profondo? Proficient breath management, freedom of articulation, balanced resonance, and skillful registration are requirements for all singers. Yet each instrument within a general *Fach* must be treated with an understanding of its own individual nature. Because of the wide diversity among singers who are termed sopranos, care must be taken not to subject them all to rigid pedagogic processes and identical performance literatures. Range and tessitura capabilities are of less importance to professional *Fach* designation than are individual voice color and the requirements of dramatic portrayal.

Categories of Soprano Voice

Although other designations are sometimes encountered, soprano voice categories are generally described as

1. soubrette
2. soubrette/coloratura
3. dramatic coloratura
4. lyric
5. lirico spinto
6. spinto
7. young dramatic (*Jugendlichdramatisch*)
8. dramatic (*Hochdramatisch*)
9. cross-*Fach* (*Zwischenfachsängerin*)

Soubrette

Perhaps the most frequently encountered female instrument belongs to the soubrette category. The term *soubrette* refers to legitimate-theater comedy roles that depict a young, frivolous, and coquettish lady's-maid who loves intrigue. By extension, soubrette serves as the designation for any actress playing such a role. Despina (*Così fan tutte*, Mozart), although she has a very high level of precocious sagacity far beyond coquetry, is a perfect example of the *soubrette intrigante* to be found in a number of opera libretti.

Light lyricism, facile agility, physical charm, and youthful appearance are essential qualities for the soubrette. Soubrette duties encompass vocal effervescence and easy melismatic negotiation over a wide range (although the soubrette is less dependent on the highest regions than is the coloratura soprano). Typical roles, in addition to Despina, are Zerlina (*Don Giovanni*, Mozart), Amore (Gluck's *Orfeo*), the Nannetta of Verdi's *Falstaff*, the Ännchens of Nicolai's *Die lustigen Weiber von Windsor* and Weber's *Der Freischütz*, Oscar (*Un ballo in maschera*, Verdi), and a host of minor characters who populate nineteenth-century opera.

In comparison with a large lyric, dramatic soprano, or contralto voice, the soubrette vocal instrument is of relatively small dimension. As an opera-theater professional, the soubrette must be of sleek physical stature as well. Nature, however, does not always produce exact accord between vocal endowment and the physical and visual requirements of the theater. It goes without saying that there are many female singers who qualify vocally as a soubrette but do not meet the theatrical expectations for that category. (A comparable problem exists for the sonorous low-voiced male who can sing an impressive King Philip [*Don Carlo*, Verdi] but whose slight physical stature makes him unbelievable in such a role.)

The soubrette voice typically bridges both light-lyric and coloratura categories. Although she is not required to have as complete an upper-range extension as her coloratura colleague, the opera soubrette is expected to manage a number of similar technical tasks. But powerful singing in her *passaggio* zone, and above it, are not part of her assignment. Although the soubrette may sing a few light coloratura roles, a great number of favorite opera roles involving coloratura are intended for a voice of considerable substance and are therefore inappropriate for the soubrette.

Persons who make casting decisions often refer to the body of lyric melismatic writing that the soubrette can successfully sing as the soubrette/coloratura *Fach*. Included among roles that are not purely soubrette in nature are a number from the nineteenth-century Italian opera buffa repertory, such as Norina (*Don Pasquale*, Donizetti), Adina (*L'elisir d'amore*, Donizetti), several protagonists of seldom-performed Bellini operas, some Rossini heroines, and, from the French literature, a role such as the Offenbach Olympia (*Les contes d'Hoffmann*). Weight and color of this singer's instrument may not make out-and-out coloratura writing favorable for her.

Dramatic Coloratura

The dramatic coloratura must display flexibility in high-lying velocity passages yet have great sustaining power. Rodelinde (*Rodelinda*, Handel), Cleopatra (*Giulio Cesare*, Handel), the Queen of the Night (*Die Zauberflöte*, Mozart), Constanze (*Die Entführung aus dem Serail*, Mozart), Semiramide (*Semiramide*, Rossini) Norma (*Norma*, Bellini), Lucia (*Lucia di Lammermoor*, Donizetti), Violetta (*La traviata*, Verdi), Abigail (*Nabucco*, Verdi), and Leonora (*Il trovatore*, Verdi), although not all of equal weight, serve as classic examples. Light soprano voices should not sing these roles; they belong to the dramatic coloratura. The role of Gilda (*Rigoletto*, Verdi) is sometimes given to the soubrette/coloratura but more appropriately belongs to the dramatic coloratura soprano (or to the facile lyric), because both flexibility and dramatic singing are required in her duets with Rigoletto and with the Duke.

Lyric

Many favorite roles in the standard repertory fall to the lyric soprano. She finds satisfying vehicles in Handel, Mozart, the bel canto composers of the first half of the nineteenth century, Verdi, Massenet, and Puccini, as well as in the works of numerous twentieth-century composers. In many ways the lyric soprano is the ideal feminine operatic voice, capable of singing such diverse roles as Susanna (*Le nozze di Figaro,* Mozart), Pamina (*Die Zauberflöte,* Mozart), Micaela (*Carmen,* Bizet), the Massenet *Manon* (which demands both power and coloratura capabilities), Tatiana (*Eugene Onegin,* Tchaikovsky—although Tatiana may fit into the spinto category as well), Marzhenka (*The Bartered Bride,* Smetana), and Mimì (*La bohème,* Puccini). Lauretta (*Gianni Schicchi,* Puccini) is frequently thought to be the property of the soubrette but actually belongs to the lyric. (Consider her duet with Rinuccio.) Liù (*Turandot,* Puccini) should be given to a lyric who has something close to spinto sustaining power; she is a light soprano only in comparison with the highly dramatic Turandot. Nedda (*I pagliacci,* Leoncavallo), Sophie (*Der Rosenkavalier,* Strauss), and Gilda (*Rigoletto,* Verdi), if the singer has sufficient coloratura skills, are lyric roles. The lyric soprano is at home in much of twentieth-century opera and in earlier nonoperatic literatures such as the Mozart Requiem; Haydn's *Die Schöpfung* and *Die Jahreszeiten;* the Bach Passions, Christmas Oratorio, and cantatas; and the less dramatic soprano roles in a number of oratorios and operas by Handel. (For additional comment regarding the Handelian repertory, see the remarks on spinto, later. Much of the literature of the mélodie and of lieder lies well for the lyric. Orchestral works like the Strauss *Vier letzte Lieder,* Barber's *Andromache's Farewell,* and a number of the Mahler songs are suitable to the substantial lyric instrument and to the lirico spinto as well.

Lirico spinto

As is clear from the preceding discussion, the designation *lyric* is flexible. Because in vocal weight the lyric soprano lies between lighter and heavier categories, a composer may ask for both lyricism and power within the same lyric role; some roles include a fair amount of coloratura writing, while others embody several spinto passages. Is the Anne of *The Rake's Progress* (Stravinsky) a lyric, or is she a peculiar blend of lyric and dramatic coloratura? Is the Floyd Susannah (*Susannah*) a lyric, or do the composer's orchestral demands push her toward spinto territory? Despite the popular "Jewel Song," is the Gounod *Faust* Marguerite, given the requirements of her final scene, really a lyric?

When the task includes a number of high, sustained tessitura passages that compete with full orchestral sound, an intermediate *Fach* is designated: lirico spinto. (The lirico spinto soprano is often paired with the lirico spinto tenor.) In much of verismo opera, even for lyric voices, being *un po' spinto* is a necessity.

Is Verdi's Desdemona, when she is called on to match Otello's *robusto* outpourings, best served by a large lyric, by a lirico spinto, or by a dramatic? Mozart's

Fiordiligi (*Così fan tutte*) must negotiate both lyrical passages and the dramatic "*Come scoglio*". Considering the orchestral writing in Dvořák's *Rusalka*, is the full role of Rusalka not too heavy for the lyric soprano who so often excerpts Rusalka's "Song to the Moon" as a contest aria?

The lieder of Schubert, Schumann, Brahms, Wolf, Mahler, and Strauss and the mélodies of Fauré, Chausson, Debussy, and Duparc offer the lyric a vast reservoir of recital material. British and American art songs are generally fully within her territory.

Although rigid rules of the older German *Fach* system are increasingly ignored in the contemporary performance world (where all voices must be of significant size), lyric voices should exercise care when moving into a neighboring heavier category, several of which are now considered.

Spinto

It is not only the heroines of Verdi and Puccini (and their nineteenth-century *verismo* contemporaries) who are called on to sing passionately and powerfully the literature that belongs to the spinto. Mozart's Vitellia (*La clemenza di Tito*) and both Donna Anna and Donna Elvira (*Don Giovanni*), despite current tendencies to cast the latter character as a flaming sex-mad lyric, are best suited to the spinto.

Aïda (*Aïda*, Verdi), Amelia (*Un ballo in maschera*, Verdi), Leonora (*La forza del destino*, Verdi), Lady Macbeth (*Macbeth*, Verdi), and Adriana (*Adriana Lecouvreur*, Cilea) are typical. Minnie (*La fanciulla del west*, Puccini), Cio-Cio-San (*Madama Butterfly*, Puccini)—who needs both dramatic vocalism and sustaining capabilities in high tessitura but who for visual reasons is sometimes sung by a coloratura— Floria (*Tosca*, Puccini), Angelica (*Suor Angelica*, Puccini), and Lady Billows (*Albert Herring*, Britten) all exhibit qualities that make their inclusion in the spinto category logical.

The Strauss Ariadne (*Ariadne auf Naxos*), Salome (*Salome*), Arabella (*Arabella*) and Chrysothemis (*Elektra*) and the Boito Margherita (*Mefistofele*) are ideal for the spinto soprano, as are most of the *verismo* soprano roles of the late nineteenth and early twentieth centuries. Soprano assignments in such concert works as the Verdi *Requiem*, Mendelssohn's *Elijah*, and Beethoven's *Ninth Symphony* can also be well handled by the spinto.

Questions arise as to who ought to sing Handel arias. (Complete performances of most Handelian operas currently are seldom undertaken.) It cannot be taken for granted that because they come from the Late Baroque, dramatic Handelian soprano arias are suited for soubrettes and lyric sopranos. A large number of the Handelian arias demand a soprano voice of sumptuous dimension. For example, "*Let the Bright Seraphim*", in which the voice competes with trumpet, is not for a lyric soprano, let alone for a soubrette. Fortunately, Handel provides an equal amount of appropriate material for both light and dramatic soprano voices. Light soprano voices should not usurp the many dramatic Handelian arias that are included in popular collections.

Jugendlichdramatisch

In the German theater, many roles of both the Italian and the German literatures are performed by a category of soprano known in Germany as the *Jugendlichdramatisch* (young dramatic). She is expected to perform the Italian spinto literature as well as to sing much of the German-language repertoire, including Agathe (*Der Freischütz*, Weber), Elsa (*Lohengrin*, Wagner), Sieglinde (*Die Walküre*, Wagner), Eva (*Die Meistersinger von Nürnberg*, Wagner), and Senta (*Der fliegende Holländer*, Wagner). (Large lyric soprano voices may also be cast as Senta.)

The Marschallin (*Der Rosenkavalier*, Strauss) is ideal for the *Jugendlichdramatisch*, even though a dramatic soprano is thought to be more appropriate by some conductors. Although the singer may, in fact, be a young developing dramatic soprano, the *Jugendlichdramatisch* category does not refer to age and does not exclude the mature performer.

Dramatic

The most ample of all soprano voices is that of the dramatic soprano. She must have great sustaining power, exhibiting both depth and brilliance of timbre as well as an imposing physical presence.

Known in the German theater as the *Hochdramatisch*, she should be able to sing the role of Santuzza (*Cavalleria rusticana*, Mascagni)—although it is equally suited to the spinto and the *Zwischenfachsängerin*—Elisabeth (*Tannhäuser*, Wagner)— which is more frequently given to the *Jugendlichdramatisch*—and most Wagnerian soprano roles, including the Brünnhildes, as well as to take on such duties as Frau (*Die Frau ohne Schatten*, Strauss), Elektra (*Elektra*, Strauss), and Turandot (*Turandot*, Puccini).

Zwischenfachsängerin

The *Zwischenfachsängerin* has a large voice with good command of low range and is most comfortable in dramatic roles that, while requiring relatively high tessitura, evade exposure of the very top of the voice for extended periods of time. She is "between categories." This type of singer is able to portray both dramatic soprano roles and some that lie within the dramatic mezzo-soprano categories, including Amneris (*Aïda*, Verdi), Lady Macbeth (*Macbeth*, Verdi), Kundry (*Parsifal*, Wagner), Ortrud (*Lohengrin*, Wagner), Santuzza (*Cavalleria rusticana*, Mascagni), and, if she is physically appropriate, the Bizet Carmen. Possessing the weight and color of the dramatic soprano, she can manage much of the same literature as the dramatic, but her most comfortable performance range is closer to that of the mezzo-soprano.

Although this volume is devoted to training soprano voices, the kinship between soprano and mezzo-soprano categories, as the well as more distantly removed rare contralto voice, must be briefly considered.

Dramatic Mezzo-Soprano

There are authorities who make no differentiation between the dramatic soprano and the dramatic mezzo-soprano. They regard the large mezzo-soprano voice as a dramatic soprano with a short top range. For them, the *Zwischenfachsängerin* and the dramatic mezzo-soprano are but subcategories of the dramatic soprano. This is too limited a viewpoint, because it does not take sufficiently into account divergent timbres nor the location of registration events that characterize categories of the female voice.

The dramatic mezzo-soprano often sings as high as and no lower than the dramatic soprano, but her timbre displays depth and the darker colors associated with tragedy, intrigue, jealousy, revenge, or outright evil intention. Examples are Eboli (*Don Carlo*, Verdi), Amneris (*Aïda*, Verdi), Azucena (*Il trovatore*, Verdi), Maddalena (*Rigoletto*, Verdi), Dalila (*Samson et Dalila*, Saint-Saëns), Charlotte (*Werther*, Massenet), Ortrud (*Lohengrin*, Wagner), Fricka (*Das Rheingold*, Wagner), Brangäne (*Tristan und Isolde*, Wagner), Herodias (*Salome*, Strauss), the Countess (*Pique Dame*, Tchaikovsky), and finally, Carmen (*Carmen*, Bizet).

The role of Carmen itself is unique, with its emphasis on charisma, physical presence, carnality, and acting ability. Because the demands of the role go beyond mere vocalism, it has been performed by a wide variety of singers, both mezzo-sopranos and sopranos. However, if the color of her voice is to match Carmen's tragic, erratic behavior, the singer cast as Carmen is ideally a dramatic mezzo-soprano. Soprano sound simply is inappropriate to Carmen, especially in the card scene and the final scene. A similar mistake is to cast a light, lyric mezzo-soprano as Carmen.

The role of Gluck's Orpheus, when not preempted by a countertenor or tenor, belongs to the dramatic mezzo-soprano, not the lyric mezzo-soprano. The dramatic mezzo-soprano is ideal for the Mahler *Das Lied von der Erde* and *Kindertotenlieder*. Because much of the lied and mélodie literature lies in middle voice, both the lyric mezzo-soprano and the dramatic mezzo-soprano find there a wealth of programmable material.

Lyric Mezzo-Soprano (Coloratura Mezzo-Soprano)

Another category of mezzo-soprano claims some of the world's greatest vocal writing: the mezzo-soprano lirico. A number of the best female opera roles from the nineteenth century are found in her domain. She is sometimes required to have greater flexibility than any other category of singer except the coloratura soprano and the *tenore di grazia*. For that reason she is designated by some sources as a mezzo-soprano coloratura. She must also play *Hosenrollen* (trouser roles), and may frequently be cast as confidante, mother, nurse, or friend of the soprano.

She has much of the rich vocal timbre of the dramatic mezzo-soprano and a rangy instrument, but without sufficient power and decibels to sing the more dramatic roles. She plays Dorabella (*Così fan tutte*, Mozart), Sextus (*La clemenza di Tito*, Mozart)—listed in the score as a contralto—Cherubino (*Le nozze di Figaro*, Mozart), Giovanna (*Anna Bolena*, Donizetti), Adalgisa (*Norma*, Bellini), Mignon (Thomas), Siebel (*Faust*, Gounod), Preziosilla (*La forza del destino*, Verdi), Hänsel (*Hänsel und Gretel*, Humperdinck), Octavian (*Der Rosenkavalier*, Strauss), and above all, the great Rossini coloratura mezzo-soprano roles, including Cenerentola—although the role of Cenerentola is assigned in the score to a contralto—and Tisbe (*La cenerentola*, Rossini), Zaida (*Il turco in Italia*, Rossini), and, culminating all such parts, Rosina (*Il barbiere di Siviglia*, Rossini). Roles such as Suzuki (*Madama Butterfly*, Puccini), Flora (*La traviata*, Verdi), and Emilia (*Otello*, Verdi), being neither patently dramatic nor lyric, are generic mezzo-soprano material as well.

The mezzo-soprano categories are mentioned here because of their musical, vocal, and dramatic importance, but they are not the subject of this book.

Contralto

The true contralto is rare. Her operatic assignments are less frequent than the roles she so readily meets in the oratorio literature. The Dritte Dame (*Die Zauberflöte*, Mozart), La Cieca (*La gioconda*, Ponchielli), Ulrica (*Un ballo in maschera*, Verdi), Dame Quickly (*Falstaff*, Verdi), Olga (*Eugene Onegin*, Tchaikovsky), the Countess (*Suor Angelica*, Puccini), Zita (*Gianni Schicchi*, Puccini), Geneviève (*Pelléas et Mélisande*, Debussy), and Madame Flora (*The Medium*, Menotti) are among her more grateful stage vehicles.

Many roles originally written for castrato are appropriate to the contralto. A host of maids, nurses, and street women belong to her. The contralto's redemption, morally and vocally, lies in the oratorio literature of Bach, Handel, and Mendelssohn, in the Baroque solo cantata, and in the lied and art-song literatures.

The contralto is mentioned here in passing in order to complete the list of vocal categories found within the female vocal world. Her special technical needs are not addressed in this work.

Not only opera and oratorio literature are considered in what follows; attention is directed to song literature as well. However, it is in the operatic literature that traditional *Fach* designations are most viable. This is the case because much of the song literature lies in a more limited range than does the operatic literature, and because vocal stamina and orchestral competition, significant aspects of opera and oratorio writing, are not as crucial to much of the song literature. In addition, much of the song literature can be performed in transposition, which is seldom the case with the opera and oratorio literatures. Indeed, an argument could be made that professional *Fach* categorization is chiefly restricted to the opera theater.

Above all, it is not the duty of the singing teacher to attempt *Fach* determination in the early stages of voice instruction. After the singer has achieved basic technical proficiency—has established vocal freedom—her voice itself will determine the *Fach*. Some teachers attempt to apply the professional Germanic *Fach* system to North

American college-age singers as though it were the prime aspect of voice pedagogy. The early discovery of registration events in a young female voice can be helpful in determining the eventual *Fach* categorization and in avoiding initial false technical and repertoire expectations. However, trying to determine the exact *Fach* for a singer of university age, female or male, mostly represents misdirected emphasis. Only when maturity and training have arrived at professional performance levels is final *Fach* determination justifiable. With that important rubric in mind, a look at registration events in female voices is appropriate.

Specific technical exercises (vocalises), most of them already in the domain of voice pedagogy, have been selected to enable the singer to accomplish tasks encountered in the performance literature for voice. In addition, numerous examples of superb vocalization material taken directly from the several categories of soprano literature are incorporated into daily systematic technical work. It is essential that brief literature excerpts supplement technical exercises.

2

Registration Events in Female Voices

Vocal REGISTRATION IS NOT THE LOCUS AT WHICH TO BEGIN ACTIVELY building systematic vocal technique: studies in registration skill belong to advanced technical work. Basic breath management, phonetic articulation, and resonance balancing must be established before a singer turns extensive attention to the registers of the singing voice. However, an awareness of the events of registration is essential to the achievement of equalization for all regions of the soprano vocal scale, especially extreme lower- and upper-range extensions. (See chapter 10 for specific exercises that deal with registration and scale equalization in all registers of soprano voices.)

In most voice pedagogies, register terminology is based on empirical sensations related to sympathetic vibration (as opposed to actual resonation) perceived in various parts of the body—for example, in the chest, in the head, and as a mixture between chest and head. Although empirically useful, traditional chest-mixture-head registration vocabulary does not correspond to verifiable resonator function. Identifiable physical and acoustic factors determine the location of register events.

Research on laryngeal structure and function supports the supposition that the range and timbre of an individual voice is in large part determined by the construction of the larynx itself (particularly the length and thickness of the vibrating vocal folds [vocal cords]), by the relationship of the larynx to adjacent structures, and by the length and configuration of the vocal tract. (The vocal tract is the resonator tube that extends from the laryngeal lips to the external lips and includes the buccal, pharyngeal, and nasal cavities; the latter are involved only in nasal continuants and foreign-language nasal vowels.) The vocal tract (resonator tube) serves as an acoustic filtering device for the laryngeally generated sound. (See fig. 2.1.) Other factors that indirectly contribute to voice classification and quality are thoracic dimension (size of the chest) and the interplay of the musculatures of the pectoral, epigastric, and abdominal areas.

Although one cannot determine voice category by external appearances, certain physical structures tend to produce specific vocal types. This is true in all of the

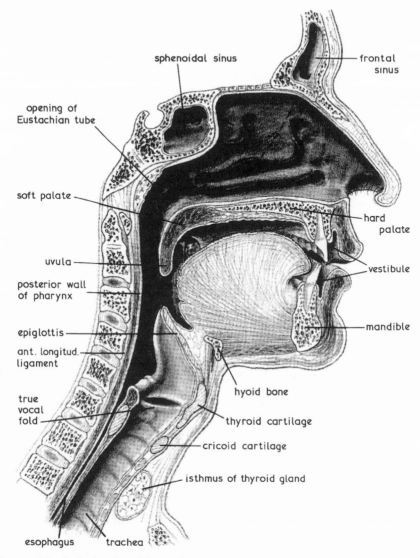

FIGURE 2.1. *Sagittal section of the vocal tract and part of the head. (Redrawn from Meribeth Bunch,* Dynamics of the Singing Voice. *[Vienna: Springer-Verlag, 1982]. By permission.)*

animal world. Based solely on the fundamental pitch the listener hears, it cannot be determined whether the barker is Lassie or Laddie. By the profundity of its bark, a normal-sized collie, a large Newfoundland, or a Saint Bernard exhibits relatively large laryngeal dimensions and capacious body structure. By contrast, if the phonating animals are of a miniature breed, both male and female have high-pitched yapping barks. Fortunately, human body structures do not differ so drastically from each

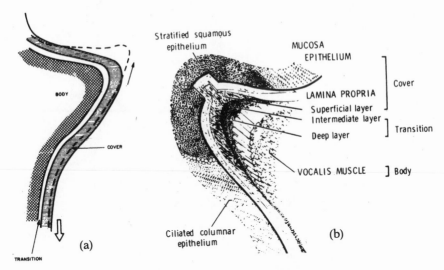

FIGURE 2.2. *Schematic cross-section of the vocal fold showing body, transition, and cover. The dashed line and upper arrow display the sliding motion that is postulated to occur between cover and body. The possibility of a vertical force on the cover is indicated by the arrow at the bottom. (b) Frontal section of a human vocal fold at the midpoint of the membranous portion, schematically presented. (From Kenneth N. Stevens and Minoru Hirano, eds.,* Vocal Fold Physiology. *[Tokyo: Tokyo University Press, 1981]. By permission.)*

other as do those of canine species. Yet it is chiefly physical factors that determine the subdivisions within the general soprano category.

A cursory discussion of the structure of the vocal folds and of the mechanism that produces pitch change is crucial for a modest but essential understanding as to why registration of the singing voice is largely determined at the level of the larynx.

As indicated in figure 2.2, the vocal fold is made up anatomically of body, transition, and cover. Graduated registration timbres are chiefly determined by degrees of activity among these components, which include the epithelium, the lamina propria, and the vocalis muscle (the body of the vocal fold). The edge of the vocal fold is sometimes called the vocal ligament. The adjustable space between the vocal folds is termed the glottis, which flexibly alters during inspiration and phonation.

Examination of the total female singing scale, from the lowest to the highest regions, shows that changes in the fundamental frequency as the pitch rises are the result of vocal-fold tensing, a procedure of elongation and thinning; conversely, lower fundamental frequencies involve a relaxing, shortening, and thickening of the folds. The cricothyroid muscles, which comprise the pars recta (upright part) and the pars obliqua (diagonal part), attach to the cricoid cartilage in front and can alter the distance between the thyroid and cricoid cartilages, thereby stretching the vocal folds longitudinally. The upper window of figure 2.3 schematically locates the

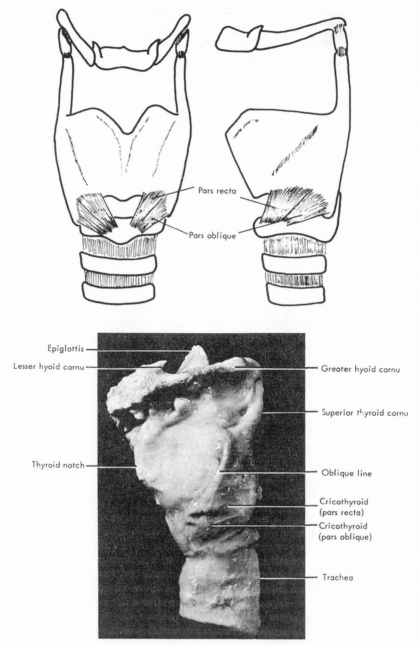

FIGURE 2.3. *Upper window: Schematic view of hyoid bone, thyroid cartilage, cricothyroid (pars recta [upright part] and pars oblique [diagonal part]), cricoid cartilage, and several tracheal rings. Lower window: Excised human larynx, showing the epiglottis, the horns of the thyroid cartilage, the thyroid notch, the pars recta and pars oblique of the cricothyroid, and the upper part of the trachea. (Redrawn from Willard R. Zemlin, ed.,* Speech and Hearing Science, *3d ed., [Englewood Cliffs, N.J.: (Prentice Hall, 1968) Allyn and Bacon, 1998]. By permission.)*

paired cricothyroid muscles between the thyroid cartilage and the cricoid cartilage; the lower window shows their position in an excised larynx. Cricothyroid activity is largely responsible for determining alterations in length and mass of the vocal folds themselves: the cricothyroid muscles, by contraction, draw the anterior part of the cricoid cartilage and the thyroid cartilage closer together, an action that lengthens, stretches, and thins the vocal folds (see figs. 2.3, 2.4, and 2.5). The vocal folds will tense if the arytenoids remain fixed. Elevation of the cricoid cartilage or forward and downward movements of the thyroid cartilage affect pitch, intensity, and voice quality. Therefore, the nature of these actions is vital in executing high range in singing, especially at and above the *secondo passaggio.*

A singer cannot consciously control the cricothyroid muscles, nor any other muscle group of the larynx, in isolation from the total laryngeal mechanism. Singing techniques that attempt to manage separate muscles of the larynx are not productive.

Laryngeal photographs of three professional singers during performance—soprano (a), soprano (b), and soprano (c)—are shown in figure 2.6. In the top series of photos, vocal-fold abduction (glottal opening during inhalation) occurs; in the bottom series, the vocal folds of each soprano display adduction (glottal approximation) for phonation.

The flexible fiberscope and the stroboscope were used to examine the three sopranos as they sang. In each photo, the epiglottis occupies the bottom region, the base of the tongue the top. The high-lying ridges that run from the epiglottis to the arytenoids are the aryepiglottic folds. Piriform sinuses are seen as dark depressions at the sides of the aryepiglottic folds. The false vocal folds, lying above the true vocal folds, are clearly visible. Although the angle of the camera and its proximity to the folds may distort some aspects of physiology, the pictures attest to the individuality of laryngeal construction, especially as regards the size and shape of the arytenoids. Despite apparent dissimilarities, all three larynges are normal.

When the laryngologist examines a patient with the laryngoscope (the laryngeal mirror), he or she sees a reverse image of the vocal folds, as indicated by the five smaller pictures of figure 2.7. The figure's three uppermost images represent (a) quiet breathing, (b) deep breathing, and (c) normal phonation. The lower section indicates (d) a form of whispering and (e) incomplete closure. A schematic illustration beneath each of the five figures displays the position of the arytenoids when the folds are (a) at rest, as in quiet breathing, (b) in complete abduction, and (c) in adduction; the schemas of (a), (b), and (c) show the movement of the arytenoids for these maneuvers.

Although comparable laryngeal muscle action occurs in both female and male phonations, there are basic physical differences between male and female larynges. Titze reports:[1]

> The overall linear dimension difference between the male larynx and the female larynx is about 20%. Furthermore, the portion of the vocal fold length

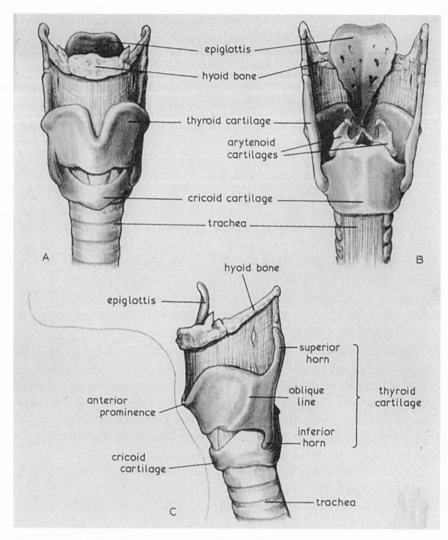

FIGURE 2.4. *Left: The hyoid bone and cartilages of the larynx. Right: Muscles of the larynx. (Redrawn from Meribeth Bunch,* Dynamic Singing *[Vienna: Springer-Verlag, 1982]. By permission.)*

that typically vibrates [the membranous length] is 60% greater in males than in females.

Significantly, then, the vibrating mass is considerably less in females than in males. Further, the entire vocal-tract length, which according to Titze is "the primary determinant for uniform scaling of formant frequencies," differs on an average of

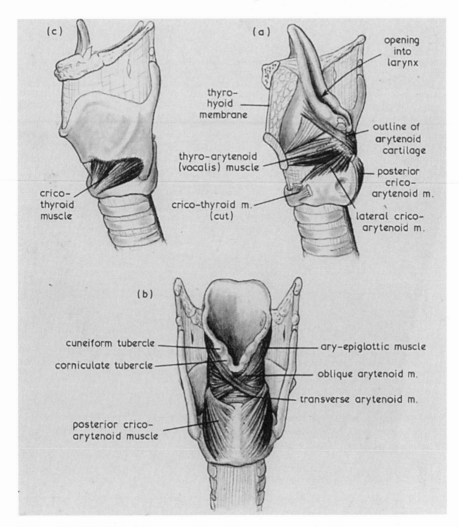

FIGURE 2.4. (*Continued*)

10–20 percent between genders. It should be noted that differences exist not only between genders, but also among generic categories of male and female voices.

The classic division of the singing scale into three registers, chest, mixed, and head, is deeply rooted in the terminology of the four major Western European schools of singing: English, French, German, and Italian. While there are varying viewpoints on register locations and their relevance to voice technique, three-register terminology flourishes wherever the art of singing is seriously pursued.

There are teachers of singing, mostly in North America, who deny the existence of registers. Others claim that the singing voice has only two registers, modal and

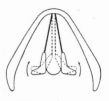

(*a*) Position of rest in quiet respiration. The intermembranous part of the rima glottidis is triangular and the intercartilaginous part is rectangular in shape.

(*b*) Forced inspiration. Both parts of the rima glottidis are triangular in shape.

(*c*) Abduction of the vocal folds. The arrows indicate the lines of pull of the posterior cricoarytenoid muscles. The abducted vocal folds and the abducted, retracted and laterally rotated arytenoid cartilages are shown in dotted outline. The entire rima glottidis is triangular.

(*d*) Adduction of the vocal folds. The arrows indicate the lines of pull of the lateral cricoarytenoid muscles. The adducted vocal folds and the medially rotated arytenoid cartilages are shown in dotted outlines.

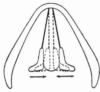

(*e*) Closure of the rima glottidis. The arrows indicate the line of pull of the transverse arytenoid muscle. Both the vocal folds and the arytenoid cartilages are adducted, but there is no rotation of the latter.

(*f*) Tension of the vocal folds, produced by the action of the cricothyroid muscles which tilt the anterior part of the cricoid cartilage upwards and so carry the arytenoid cartilages backwards.

(*g*) Relaxation of the vocal folds, produced by the action of the thyroarytenoid muscles, which draw the arytenoid cartilages forwards.

FIGURE 2.5. *A series of diagrams showing different positions of the vocal folds and the arytenoid cartilages. (From 37th Brit. ed. edited by Robert Warwick and Peter Williams, eds.,* Gray's Anatomy, *[London: W. B. Saunders, 1980]. By permission.)*

falsetto; they echo the terminology of voice science, which, while adequate for explaining the events of the speaking voice, fails to take into account the extended regions of the voice of singing. Still others make additional subdivisions among the three classically designated registers.

The degree of vocal ligament vibration, or, conversely, the extent to which the vocalis muscle is involved, influences timbre nuances, among the "head," "mixed," and "chest" registers. As mixed timbre increases in the direction of heavier chest function, the role of the vocalis muscle (the more internal segment of the vocal fold) grows; the opposite occurs as the singer leaves chest timbre for mixed voice and head voice. The cricothyroids contract as pitch ascends, offering greater resistance to the thyroarytenoids. The long soprano middle range exhibits a dynamic muscle equilibrium between chest and head functions. In head timbre, action is centered more on the elongated vocal ligament itself.

A   B   C

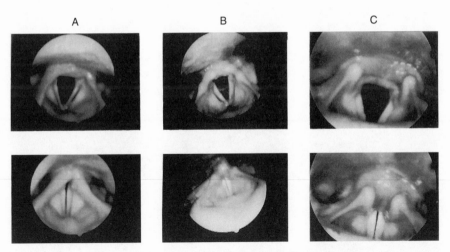

FIGURE 2.6. *Stroboscopic views of vocal-fold abduction and adduction from three professional sopranos during singing. (Otto B. Schoepfle Vocal Arts Center, Oberlin Conservatory of Music, 1998)*

Register demarcation events help identify voice category. For the typical lyric soprano voice, the traditional registration pivotal point between the chest voice and the long mixed voice (*voce media*) is located a minor third above the keyboard's middle C (C_4) at $E\flat_4$. This region of mixed voice for the lyric soprano is regarded in most pedagogies (including this one) as extending upward from $E\flat_4$ to $F\sharp_5$ or G_5 and, for some singers, with a noticeable registration subdivision at C_5 or $C\sharp_5$, most marked in sizable soprano voices; lower-middle mixed voice extends from $E\flat_4$ to $C\sharp_5$; upper-middle mixed voice from $C\sharp_5$ to $F\sharp_5$. Beyond $F\sharp_5$, at pitches ranging through C_6 (high C) or $C\sharp_6$, lies the distinct head voice. (See fig. 2.8.) Although these identifiable regions of timbre are traditional, it is possible to carry head voice downward throughout most of the scale.

The *passaggi* of the singing voice are not necessarily related to keyboard pitches. For example, the soprano's upper *passaggio* may lodge on the sharp or on the flat side of $F\sharp_5$; the same is true of the lower $E\flat_4$ *passaggio*. The upper *passaggio* of a light soprano voice may be exactly at $F\sharp_5$ or may lean toward G_5, while in the heavier soprano voice it may be located on the low side of $F\sharp_5$, almost at F_5. In large soprano voices, the lower *passaggio* is generally closer to E_4 than to $E\flat_4$. As Figure 2.8 indicates, for the mezzo-soprano and the contralto these events occur at other points in the scale.

A soprano (particularly if she has a relatively large instrument) may be aware of the progressive registration action that marks entry into her upper middle range ($C\sharp_5$–$F\sharp_5$). Because she experiences gradual differences in sympathetic vibration and in energy levels between $C\sharp_5$ and $F\sharp_5$, she may assume that her upper *passaggio* lies

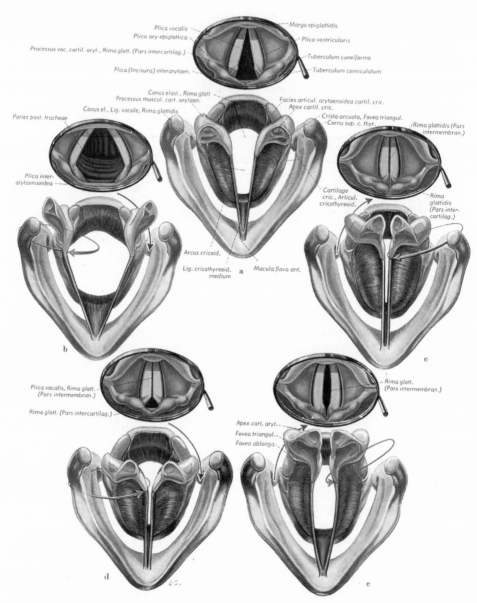

FIGURE 2.7. *Five laryngoscopic views of the vocal folds, with a schematic diagram beneath each:* (a) quiet breathing, (b) deep inhalation, (c) normal phonation, (d) a form of whispering, and (e) incomplete closure. *(From E. Pernkopf,* Atlas der topographischen und angewandten Anatomie des Menschen, *ed. H. Ferner, vol. 1 [Munich: Urban & Schwarzenberg, 1963]. By permission.)*

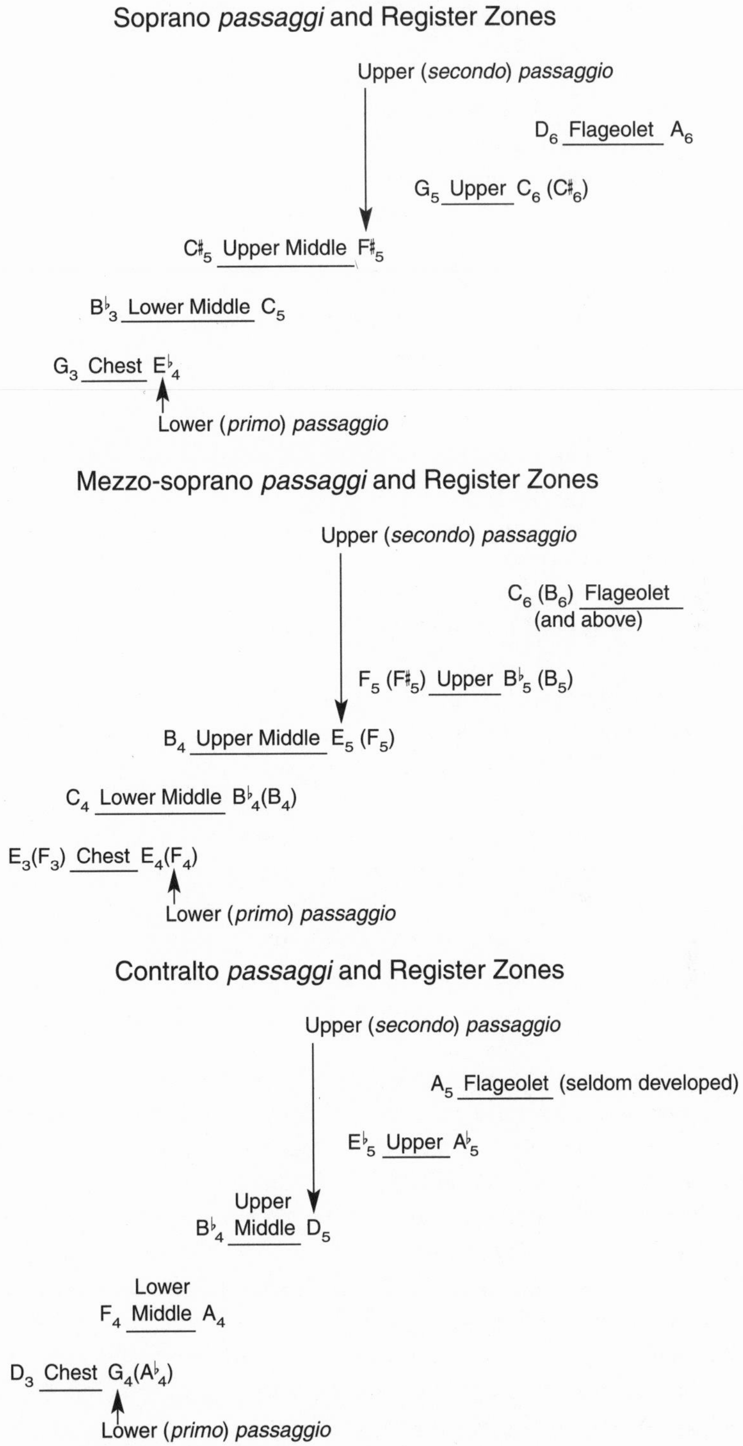

Soprano *passaggi* and Register Zones

Upper (*secondo*) *passaggio*

D₆ Flageolet A₆

G₅ Upper C₆ (C♯₆)

C♯₅ Upper Middle F♯₅

B♭₃ Lower Middle C₅

G₃ Chest E♭₄

Lower (*primo*) *passaggio*

Mezzo-soprano *passaggi* and Register Zones

Upper (*secondo*) *passaggio*

C₆ (B₆) Flageolet
(and above)

F₅ (F♯₅) Upper B♭₅ (B₅)

B₄ Upper Middle E₅ (F₅)

C₄ Lower Middle B♭₄(B₄)

E₃(F₃) Chest E₄(F₄)

Lower (*primo*) *passaggio*

Contralto *passaggi* and Register Zones

Upper (*secondo*) *passaggio*

A₅ Flageolet (seldom developed)

E♭₅ Upper A♭₅

Upper
B♭₄ Middle D₅

Lower
F₄ Middle A₄

D₃ Chest G₄(A♭₄)

Lower (*primo*) *passaggio*

FIGURE 2.8. Passaggi *and register zones in female voices.*

25

at $E^\flat_5$ or E_5. This is because the lengthening of the vocal folds increases slightly but steadily from $C^\sharp_5$ to $F^\sharp_5$. However, it is at $F^\sharp_5$ where most sopranos encounter a more discernible shift in energization and vowel modification.

Some techniques of singing are built on the conscious separation of registers, independently carrying chest, then head, throughout the scale. In register-separation systems, the singer strives to develop the "heavy mechanism" (greater vocalis muscle dependence), purposely disconnecting it from the "light mechanism" (vocal ligament focus) by carrying the heavier timbre as far as possible into the upper range. According to this premise, the two "mechanisms" will then be reunited at some future moment. However, register unification that produces an even scale is physiologically not achievable through register violation. The pedagogic aim should be to unite the registers, not to separate them.

Despite the fact that register separation techniques are potentially damaging to healthy functioning of the voice, register violation is considered acceptable, even desirable, in some popular and ethnic singing styles. The appointment calendar of today's laryngologist who deals with the singing voice is heavily weighted with pop singers (the "untrained professional voice") who carry chest voice well into upper range.

Classical singers who have been taught to separate the vocal registers also develop segmented ranges and an inability to achieve a graduated musical scale. Laryngeal damage caused by register-separation maneuvers makes future register unification difficult; one set of muscle responses has won a permanent victory over the other.

The $E^\flat_4$ pivotal registration point referred to above—the classic dividing pitch between chest and mixed registers—is sometimes referred to as "the Melba point," because of the insistence of the Australian soprano Helen Porter Armstrong (better known as Dame Nellie Melba) that chest timbre not be permitted beyond that point.[2] As has been seen, the vocal folds—part of the thyroarytenoid muscle complex—are thickest in the lowest pitches of the voice; as the fundamental rises, the folds engage in the tensing, thinning, and elongating process mentioned above. Attempting to maintain the mass of the vocal folds while stretching their length during pitch elevation invites imbalances among internal and external laryngeal musculatures, causing hyperfunction (excessive activity) in one muscle group and hypofunction (insufficient activity) in another. In traditional voice pedagogy, this kind of heavy timbre is pejoratively described as "carrying up chest voice." There is, however, no danger in "carrying down head voice." These dicta, enunciated by a great soprano of the not-so-distant past and in accordance with historic tradition, are fully supported by modern physical and acoustic evidence.

Although the classical singer must strenuously avoid techniques that violate register function (carrying chest voice upward beyond its natural boundaries), there are four kinds of voice timbre a soprano has available for selection in her lower range (from approximately $E^\flat_4$ downward). They are dependent on the graduated adjustments of the laryngeal muscles and on resonator responses to those actions. Understanding their mechanical source helps the soprano to avoid unhealthy registration practices.

These four female timbres can best be described in the traditional terms of voice pedagogy:

1. head
2. head-chest mixture
3. chest-head mixture
4. chest (also termed pure, open, or raw)

In making the decision to introduce chest mixtures below the Melba point (generally E^b_4) in response to a tonal concept that is beyond direct physical control, the singer changes the relationship of the cricothyroid muscles to the thyroarytenoid and cricoarytenoid muscles. The deeper, interior portion of the vocal fold, the vocalis muscle, relaxes with the shortening of the vocal folds. (See figs. 2.3, 2.4, and 2.5.) When a female chooses some form of chest-head mixture, inasmuch as the vocalis muscle is relaxed, greater longitudinal tension can take place in the vocal ligament itself, thereby raising the fundamental pitch. The vocal folds elongate as the cricothyroids contract. Mixed voice is a constantly flexible dance between these functions. In head voice, as vocal-fold elongation takes place, vibration is concentrated to a greater extent on the vocal ligament.

Laryngeal action and resonator shaping contribute to the registration of the singing voice. Registers are experienced by the performer as vibratory sensations located in the chest or head. However, trying to place the voice in the chest or head is counterproductive to dynamic (as opposed to static) laryngeal action. Airflow turned into tone by the vibrating larynx cannot be directed to some particular part of the resonator system.

Above C_6 or $C^\#_6$, another timbre, called flageolet, is identifiable. A further extension of head voice, flageolet is a quality somewhat distinguishable from the rest of head voice. Many sopranos can produce flageolet in extreme regions of the scale, not infrequently as high as G_7, A^b_7, or even a semitone or two beyond. In rare cases, flageolet is operative up to C_8 and (increasingly rarely) slightly beyond. It is mostly laryngeal size and structure that determine the limitations of this upper-range extension: the smaller the instrument, the greater the probability of demonstrating extreme flageolet function. (Mezzo-soprano and contralto registration pivotal events occur at lower points in the scale, so flageolet technique is a lesser option, especially for the contralto [see fig. 2.8].)

Because of the nature of professional performance literature for the soprano, she often must sing in an extended portion of her upper range. In the early phase of vocal training she may encounter difficulty in this region, because the graduated tensing (thinning and elongation of the vocal folds) noticeably increases with ascending pitch, requiring greater skill and additional breath energy. At a certain point in the mounting scale, as fundamental pitch rises and breath energy increases, cricothyroid muscle activity reaches its structural limit.

After the lengthening process for pitch determination has reached its physical boundaries, additional semitones may be accomplished through increasing vocal-fold tension. However, this latter maneuver is to be avoided, because the inner elastic tissues of the vocal folds are not constructed to sustain stressful action over long periods of time without damage. Damping (also termed dampening), which produces the flageolet voice, assists in avoiding excessive vocal-fold stress as the head voice of the soprano is extended upward to its fullest vocal-fold extension. Damping effects a decrease in the scope of vocal-fold movement: only the fold's anterior is set into rapid vibration. (See chapter 10 for a series of practical exercises.)

In summary, it is the relationship of vocalis-muscle tension to passive tension in the vocal ligament that produces the subtle changes involved in transitions among chest, mixed, head and flageolet timbres. Ability to use the colors of registration stems from habituated tonal concepts originating in the musicianly mind, not from conscious attempts at direct mechanical control.

As an acoustic filtering device, the vocal tract (from the glottis to the lips) reacts to the altering laryngeal source with corresponding resonance responses (see chapters 6, 7, and 8). Vocal registration, then, is neither solely laryngeal nor purely supraglottic, but both. It is also dependent on subglottic pressure and airflow ratios, subjects to be discussed later.

The classification of voices and the literature to be selected for them in performance are largely dependent on the size of the vocal instrument and on the points in the musical scale at which registration events for that particular voice category occur. Registration undergirds vocal instruction in all of its dimensions. Knowledge of the basic physiology of vocal registration must guide the pedagogue throughout both early and advanced instruction. It should be reiterated that wise pedagogy does not introduce the specifics of registration to the student at an early stage.

The question as to when voice study should begin must now be disposed of before turning to practical measures for achieving a solid vocal technique.

3

Making a Beginning

W‍HEN SHOULD INDIVIDUAL VOICE INSTRUCTION BEGIN? AS SOON AS there is an interest in singing. The larynx undergoes changes at puberty. It might seem logical to delay singing instruction until after that event. However, if a child wishes to sing, that child will sing. At any age, no matter how young, she can be helped to better voice production if breath management is efficient, vowels are clearly defined, and laryngeal tensions are eliminated.

The problem in teaching a child to sing is not that the prepubescent larynx is fragile but that the demands put on it may be inadvertently excessive. Children should not be expected to sing in the same ranges, with the same intensity, or for the same periods of time as adults. If a child is taught according to sensible physiologic and acoustic principles, her early years of training will contribute to a favorable instructional continuum, and she will move quickly forward as a young adult singer. A number of highly successful performers have sung extensively during early childhood. But the nature of instruction given a child is crucial. Many adult singers suffer from malfunctional habits ingrained by inexpert voice instruction they received during childhood. Some persons who as children participated in popular children's choirs later have had difficulty in managing the adult singing voice. It is not improbable that success or failure for a number of singers can be attributed, at least in part, to the way they were asked to produce vocal sound as children.

As with the male larynx, the larynx of the female continues to undergo mutation after puberty, but far less radically. It is logical for females to begin private voice study around age fourteen. By then, as well as exhibiting better vocal stability than most adolescent males, many female adolescents show a greater level of general maturity. If a youngster adheres to several basic principles, there is no reason for her not to sing during pubertal change (unless she experiences discomfort). Those principles are that

1. she remain chiefly in middle range, avoiding both low and high tessitura extremes, with only occasional modest exploration of upper and lower ranges,

2. she not attempt high-decibel intensity levels, and
3. she not sing too long at a time.

Evidence regarding later effects of early vocal training on both adult female and male students is hard to establish, because regardless of when they began to sing, some singers exhibit inherent vocal talent and stamina, while others do not. The young person will benefit if good vocal production is induced and if general musicianship is developed.

One reason for encouraging voice lessons as soon as age fourteen is that the performance urge is often present at that age, and because opportunities abound for unmonitored vocal activities that are patently injurious to young female voices. Some of these take place in popular ensembles and "show choirs," some in self-generated teenage troupes modeled on lucrative but vocally destructive pop-music styles. It is well known that young persons—and some not so young—with limited or no vocal training can overnight become stars in the entertainment world. Their success may not be based on inherent vocal beauty, skill, or unusual musical talent, but on pop-music market criteria. Teen-age women often get involved in contemporary gospel or emotive religious choruses, activities that often rely on heavy vocalis-muscle participation. Even if a sturdy larynx has been able to minimize the effects of early vocal abuse, time lost in correcting ingrained malfunction is a serious impediment to later development.

Those who deal with the classically trained singing voice are sometimes accused of elitism. But it is not just the desire to accomplish a technique surpassing the normal ability of nonprofessional voice users that drives historic voice pedagogy. Classic voice technique is based on a centuries-old artistic canon of the Western world stemming from ancient Greece: beauty, strength, and health. These criteria are absent from many pop and ethnic styles of singing. By reducing the incidence of detrimental vocal-fold activity, harmful practices found in many pop-vocal idioms can be diminished. Teachers of nonclassical styles often teach performers who are aware that they have voice problems but who do not want to turn out sounding like opera singers. The voice instructor's task is not to denigrate the worth of a popular idiom, nor even to attempt to change the student's repertory, but to find ways to minimize injurious practices. Pop singers may never arrive at timbres considered appropriate to classical singing styles (nor is that their aim), but by improving breath management, laryngeal response, and resonance balance, they can approach safer vocal production. Because professional voice training is largely directed to the art song, the Lied, the mélodie, the oratorio, and the opera, this book deals mainly with those literatures.

Particularly on the North American continent, young singers who want to have professional careers generally enroll at age eighteen in a university school of music or a conservatory of music. This happens less frequently in Europe, where serious voice study often commences a few years later, at the completion of university study.

But the beginning soprano is not always an early teen-ager or young adult. In both Europe and North America, the noninstitutional teacher has students who discover a midlife or even later interest in voice study. How does one approach their differing chronological circumstances?

Physical aging varies immensely, particularly with regard to the vocal instrument and to what it has undergone by way of healthy activity, misuse, or abuse. A woman of thirty-five will have certain advantages over her studio mate of eighteen. But if she has previously sung only for pleasure, she will probably have to contend with layers of acquired bad vocal habits. She may also find it difficult to be a beginner among younger beginners.

Regardless of age, everyone has the right to sing. But the mature singer will require as much time to learn to sing as does the younger woman. For a thirty-five-year-old soprano to begin voice study in the hope of singing professionally is impractical; a professional performance goal is unrealistic for the older beginner.

What of the aging voice? A number of teachers find rewarding work in instructing the elderly. The human larynx undergoes change along with the rest of the body (see appendix), but it is never too late to study voice, so long as it is recognized that professionalism is not in the picture for the older singer.

Skillful singing at a professional level is seldom accomplished by anyone within the period of a few years. Just as it is difficult to cite a concert pianist who began the study of piano at age thirty-five or a violinist of note who started late in adulthood, so is it with the singer. Indeed, by their mid-twenties, most professional singers have already begun their careers at some level—in preprofessional training programs or engagements. Avocational as opposed to vocational goals ought to be clear to both teacher and student. The private voice teacher must be prepared to deal with the entire gamut of age and to sort out the students' intentions.

4

Breath Energy in Singing

Technical problems in singing are traceable to acoustic and physiologic sources. The task of the teacher of singing is to diagnose what is amiss and to prescribe corrective measures in precise language. Without specificity of language, only hit-or-miss information can be delivered to the student.

The functions of the tripartite vocal instrument (motor, vibrator, and resonator) are interdependent and cannot be isolated from each other. Yet all discernible interruptions of good voice function fit into one of these areas, and each must be separately addressed. Numerous exercises that make up a long-range comprehensive technical system are proposed for the alleviation of specific problems. It is not intended that all of the exercises of one area be accomplished before turning to the next. To allow for assimilation by mind and body, a few patterns from each segment, including those based on passages from the literature, should be practiced equally. While alternating one technical area with another, the whole system is eventually to be covered.

Breath management is the essential foundation for all skillful vocalism. (The traditional term "support" is avoided here because it can have many meanings, depending on the pedagogic system.) Breath management for singing is best achieved by preserving a "noble" position that permits interplay among the muscles of the upper chest, the ribcage area, and the anterolateral abdominal wall. Voice pedagogy of the historic Italian school (which largely formed the basis of professional vocalism in the nineteenth and the first half of the twentieth centuries, and which continues to flourish among most premier singers today) and modern scientific investigation both lend support to the notion that breath is the power source for the singing voice. The internationally recognized *appoggio* (from *appoggiare*, to lean against, to be in contact with) is a form of breath-management coordination that must be learned if the singer is to unite energy and freedom for successfully meeting the tasks of professional vocalism. The term *breath energy* refers to the results of *appoggio* coordination.

The *appoggio* is based on substantiated physical fact. We live under atmospheric pressure. At inspiration, downward contraction of the diaphragm and an expansion

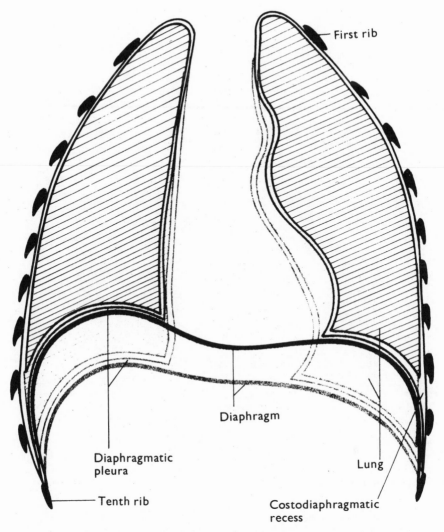

First rib

Diaphragm

Diaphragmatic
pleura

Lung

Tenth rib

Costodiaphragmatic
recess

FIGURE 4.1. *An outline drawing showing the change in thoracic shape resulting from downward contraction of the diaphragm. (From J. G. Romanes, ed.,* Cunningham's Manual of Practical Anatomy, *Vol. 2, 14th ed. [Oxford: Oxford University Press, 1977]. By permission.)*

of the intercostals increase the volume of the lungs. But diaphragmatic action is often misunderstood. It should be kept in mind that the central tendon of the diaphragm is attached to the pericardium, in which the heart is housed, and that diaphragmatic descent is far less drastic than many singers have been given to believe (see fig. 4.1). Nor is the diaphragm locally controllable. It becomes basically passive during expiration and phonation.

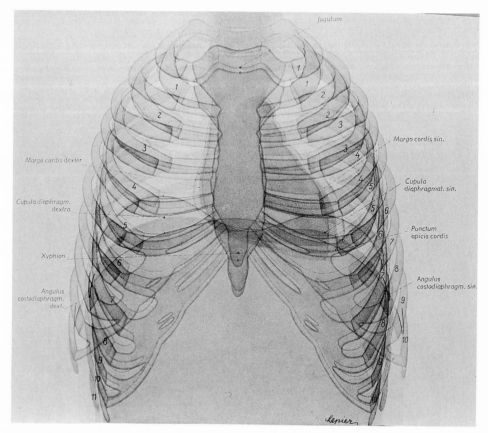

FIGURE 4.2. *A schematic representation based on X-ray studies of the positions of the sternum, ribcage, and diaphragm during several phases of the breath cycle. (From E. Pernkopf,* Atlas der topographischen und angewandten Anatomie des Menschen, *ed. H. Ferner. Munich: Urban & Schwarzenberg, 1963. By permission.)*

At inspiration, as air freely enters the respiratory tract, the pressure below the glottis (subglottic pressure) becomes lower than the atmospheric pressure. As we exhale, speak, cry, laugh, call, or sing (all encompassed in the term *phonation*), pressures within the lung (the intrapleural and intrapulmonary pressures) begin to rise, reaching a point of equilibrium with atmospheric pressure. Then, as phonation is extended (or as expiration occurs), subglottic pressure continues to rise until it reaches a point well beyond the level of atmospheric pressure, at which moment the diaphragm is in its most elevated position. (See fig. 4.2.) One again inhales in order to renew the oxygen supply and to recommence the cycle.

Three diaphragmatic positions are indicated in figure 4.2. When the sternum is in a relatively high position, the ribcage has its greatest expansion, and the diaphragm its lowest. As subglottic pressure rises, it equalizes with atmospheric pressure; the sternum begins to lower, and the diaphragm arrives at a medium position. When the sternum falls, the cage collapses, and the diaphragm ascends to its highest location. These phenomena are common to the breath cycle during spoken phonation but should be modified for singing. *Appoggio* singing technique avoids the rapid collapse experienced in customary breathing or in normal speech by retaining the inspiratory posture of the sternum and the ribcage for longer durations, thereby retarding diaphragmatic ascent.

Excessive subglottic pressure in singing is undesirable. Typical mounting subglottic pressure is best minimized by avoiding any overload of airflow, both at inspiration and during phonation. The vocal folds ought to offer neither more nor less resistance to subglottic pressure than is appropriate to the phonatory task at hand.

Management of the breath for singing must be adroitly controlled by dynamic intensity and by the natural phonetic action of the vocal tract, which, lying above the vocal folds, acts as a filter for the laryngeally generated sound. Proctor succinctly describes this process:[1] "Subglottic pressure combined with effective use of the supraglottic resonators is the primary factor determining vocal intensity."

Lung volume is measurable. The capacity of the lung, measured through forced expiration (sudden rapid breath expulsion) following full inspiration, is termed *vital capacity*. *Tidal breath* consists of air that can be inhaled and exhaled in quiet breathing. *Complemental breath* is air that may be taken in addition to tidal breath but requires additional inspiratory activity. What remains in the lung after full expiration is termed *residual air*. (The lung can never be completely emptied.) When in a state of repose, breathing in and out, we make use only of tidal breath. By contrast, professional singing may call upon most of the vital capacity of the lung.

The rate of breath emission relies on the synergistic work among the larynx, elastic lung forces, and the muscles of the torso. Titze describes the process:

> If phonation occurs during the expiratory process, the flow of air is relatively small because the respiratory tract is constricted by the nearly closed glottis. . . . Lung pressure can vary greatly over the [respiratory] cycle . . . which would normally cause major fluctuations in the airflow. By varying the glottis continuously (more closure for higher pressures and less closure for lower pressures) the pulmonary system can regulate the flow of air to be more constant. This regulation, which is accomplished autonomically by the nervous system, applies to both inspiration and expiration. . . . [L]aryngeal action and thoracic action are not independent. There are reflexes that tie them together into a functional unit.

Volume in the lung is controlled partly by intra-abdominal pressures below the diaphragm (which separates the respiratory system from the digestive system) and partly by what happens above the diaphragm; interacting forces of the lungs and of the chest wall determine changes in lung volume and in subglottic pressure. This action is further described by Proctor as "the balance between a lung elastic force in an expiratory direction, and a chest elastic force in an inspiratory direction."[3]

Neither physical exertion nor excessive energy produces skillful singing. However, beginning singers of all ages tend to use energy levels befitting folklike phonation. The normal breath cycle appropriate to speech is not identical to that required for singing. With regard to airflow, vocal-fold response, and resonation, the tasks of skillful singing require higher rates of breath energy than those of speech. (Yet the high levels of subglottic pressure that tend to occur in range extension must be kept in check.) In meeting the demands of artistic singing, air emission should be paced over longer periods of time and at different intensity levels than in speech.

Elongation of the breath cycle for singing is dependent on a learned technique (*appoggio*) that results from the concerted action on diaphragmatic movement by the muscles of the thorax and the abdominal wall, the latter comprising the transverse abdominis (transversus abdominis), the internal oblique (obliquus internus abdominis), the external oblique (obliquus externus abdominis) and the rectus abdominis (see figs. 4.3 and 4.4). The musculature of the thoracic cage, together with the abdominal musculature, can be coordinated so as to retard or accelerate reflex expiratory action. Then the duration of the breath cycle is not solely dependent on reflexive diaphragmatic or intercostal activity, as is normally the case in the non-phonatory breath cycle or in spoken phonation.

The diaphragm is activated during inspiration, then becomes largely passive during phonation. Limited recent research suggests that the passivity of the diaphragm in extended expiration may be less marked than earlier research indicated. In any event, the basic function of the diaphragm remains involuntary, with contraction occurring on inhalation and passivity at expiration. However, control over the muscles of the abdominal wall *can* be learned. Much of the technique of breath management in singing is directed toward retarding the expiratory phase of the breath cycle.

During the normal breath cycle, the intercostal muscle groups (extrinsic and intrinsic) assist in altering subglottic pressure: the external intercostal muscles elevate the ribs, operating in an inspiratory gesture; the internal intercostals subsequently draw the ribs inward in an expiratory gesture. Their behavior is coordinated with diaphragmatic and ribcage movements and is not locally controllable. Subglottic pressure is additionally regulated by the response of the vocal folds to air emission. (The vocal folds are parted for inspiration, then approximated—moved toward each other—for the closure phase that produces phonation.) In a sighing maneuver the breath exits quickly, whereas in grunting (the result of pressed phonation) the larynx dams up the breath through its valvular powers of resistance, holding back the flow of air. Letting go of this breath damming yields the audible grunt. Some techniques of singing are built on the sigh (high air flow), even advising that sung phonation should take place following consciously induced depletion of the air supply. An opposing technique is based on excessive glottal closure (breath damming). In

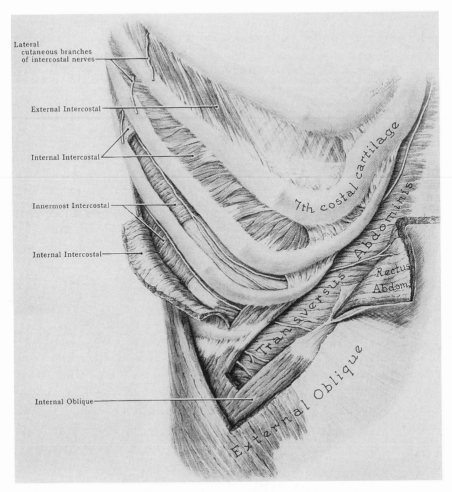

FIGURE 4.3. *The intercostals, lower ribs, and muscles of the abdomen, showing the common direction of the fibers of the external intercostal and external oblique muscles and the continuity of the internal intercostal with the internal oblique muscles at the anterior ends of the 9th, 10th, and 11th intercostal spaces. (Redrawn from J. C. Boileau Grant, An Atlas of Anatomy, 5th ed. [Baltimore: Williams & Wilkins Company, 1962]. By permission.)*

the international professional singing world, sighing, minimal breath, or grunting maneuvers do not play an acceptable role in balanced voice production.

To be skillful, a voice user must learn to maintain equilibrium between the mechanics of airflow regulation and vocal-fold resistance to the air in order to accomplish precise coordination between the two. The task is to develop dynamic, as opposed to static, equilibrium over this aerodynamic-myoelastic instrument (airflow and muscle response to the airflow). It is not the job of the singer to see how large a

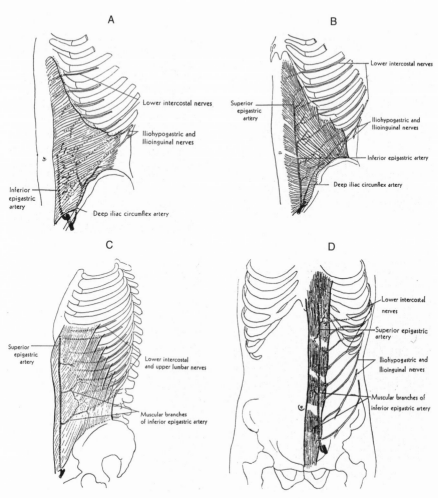

FIGURE 4.4. *Muscles of the thorax and abdomen: (a) transversus abdominis; (b) obliquus internus abdominis; (c) obliquus externus abdominis; (d) rectus abdominis. (From Daniel P. Quiring and John H. Warfel,* The Head, Neck and Trunk *[Philadelphia: Lea & Febiger, 1967]. By permission.)*

volume of air can be inhaled and expelled during the singing of a phrase, nor is it advisable to conceive of the diaphragm as a piston that drives air upward to the larynx. It should be emphasized that there is no way in which a singer can consciously exercise *direct* mechanical control over the diaphragm.

The lungs supply the larynx with breath. The column of exiting air does not originate in the pelvic or abdominal areas, to be directed upward by the lower abdomen in order to feed the larynx—air is already present in the trachea, ready for immediate use. It does not occupy spaces below the lungs; "belly breathing" is an unachievable aim. The goal of efficient breath-management technique is not to try to sing on a column of breath that starts in the region of the navel, but to allow the exiting tracheal air to be turned into tone through appropriate degrees of natural phonatory resistance offered by the vibrating vocal folds. The entire process is stabilized by the *appoggio,* which indeed does have its source in the antagonist musculature of the abdominal wall (the transverse abdominis, internal oblique, external oblique, and rectus abdominis muscles; see figs. 4.3 and 4.4). Motor activity of the breath mechanism for singing goes beyond that required for speech. The *appoggio* method of breath management maintains for longer periods of time the natural inspiratory antagonism among the muscles of the abdominal wall. In singing (during which the motor activity of the breath mechanism is greater than in spoken phonation), the initial antagonism of the major muscles of the abdominal wall—which occurs more fully in deep than in shallow inspiration—is maintained far longer than in speaking. The *appoggio* method of breath management relies on the natural antagonism among these muscles at the inspiratory moment of the breath cycle.

These abdominal muscles are layered one over the other. The transversus abdominis (so called because of the direction of its fibers and its lateral location across the abdomen) is the innermost muscle of the abdominal wall. It has its origins in the pelvic and iliac (hip) regions; its lower fibers, with insertions in the lowest six ribs, curve downward and laterally. The internal oblique muscle lodges over the transversus abdominis and immediately under the external oblique. The posterior fibers of the internal oblique run upward and laterally and insert into the lower borders of the bottom three or four ribs and the internal intercostals. Together with the transverse abdominis, some of the fibers of the internal oblique insert into the pubic crest; the other fibers of the two muscles fuse together. Some of their fibers unite in an abdominal sheath, blending with the external oblique muscle. The upper parts of this sheath attach to the seventh, eighth, and ninth ribs.

The external oblique is the largest and the most superficial (closest to the external surface of the torso) of these important flat abdominal muscles. It arises from the external surfaces and bottom borders of the lowest eight ribs. (It should be kept in mind that the fifth rib is at the level of the nipple; although the female mammary gland may not rest at the fifth rib, it originates there.) Attached to the cartilages of corresponding ribs, the external oblique muscle runs downward and backward. However, it is somewhat loosely connected to the transverse and internal oblique sheath. The low dorsal region of the thoracic cage (eleventh and twelfth ribs) is as important in managing the breath as are the front ten ribs.

The transversus abdominis, internal oblique, and external oblique are the three chief players in the *appoggio* technique. A fourth muscle, the rectus abdominis, a long, flat muscle that runs the entire length of the front of the abdomen, courses from the pubic region to the xiphoid process (lowest point) of the sternum and inserts into the fifth, sixth, and seventh ribs. The rectus abdominis is a member of the abdominal sheath that includes the internal oblique, the external oblique, and the transverse abdominis, but its role in breath management during singing is not as important as those played by the other three large abdominal muscles. Systems of breath management for singing that are based on localized control over the rectus abdominis (especially at the epigastric level) overlook the deeper center of control on which the *appoggio* is based.

For the tasks of singing it is necessary to retain the inspiratory gesture as long as possible and to reduce the increase of subglottic pressure that normally occurs during the expiratory gesture. Reduction of excessive air flow and of accumulating subglottic pressure is achieved by remaining as long as possible in the inspiratory position. Especially during singing, the muscles of the torso must be routined to delay customary expiratory movement, thereby retarding the recoil action of the lungs. Such coordination avoids displacement of the sternum, collapse of the ribcage, and rapid diaphragmatic mounting.

Another factor remains to be further considered: the position of the torso itself. The sternum must be in a comfortably elevated posture *prior to inspiration* to allow full rib expansion and to retain the axial posture that avoids high-chest breathing. (High-chest breathing takes place when the sternum is low, not when the sternum is elevated.) If the sternum falls, the ribs move rapidly inward, and the diaphragm rises more quickly. There should be no (or at least minimal) chest displacement during inhalation, phonation, and breath renewal.

The two focal points, then, for arriving at the noble posture essential to the maintenance of the *appoggio* are the sternum and the pelvic-hip region. The body assumes the linear alignment of head and neck (offering external frame support for the larynx), torso, hips, and legs.

Although it is not the actual positioning of the feet and the legs that controls axial balance, the weight of the body should be directed to the balls of the feet, not to the heels. Weight can either shift from one leg and buttock to the other or be equally balanced on both legs. Any static postural setting is to be avoided; the possibility of shifting the weight of the body must be constantly present, even when the singer remains in stationary posture. Dynamic bearing, in contrast to static positioning among the head, neck, chest, and pelvis, permits freedom in both the axial and the appendicular body—arms and hands, legs and feet.

Groups of muscles not directly associated with respiration provide a structural support for the breath mechanism. They consist of the trapezius, the sternocleidomastoids, the serratus, and the latissimus dorsi muscles. When the head is properly a part of this axis, the larynx itself, being neither elevated nor thrust forward, is well supported by the external muscular frame structure of the neck, comprising the sternocleidomastoid, scalenus, and capitis and the upper portion of the trapezius.

Developing the ability to increase the duration of the breath cycle necessary for masterful singing is the most important discipline in technical study. The process can be accelerated by systematically building *appoggio* coordination with methodical training of the inspiratory muscles through repeated brief onset patterns, renewing immediately at the moment of release the small amount of breath used for the production of each onset. Short onset exercises drill the capacity to remain in a stable position during the cycle of phonation and breath renewal. As the musculatures of the abdominal, pectoral, and nuchal—back of the neck—regions develop through use and as coordination between the larynx and the breath motor increases, the duration of the phonatory periods can be extended.

Following proper onset, the release-inhalation maneuver silently reestablishes the original low level of subglottic pressure. Almost no displacement of the musculature of the abdominal wall occurs. In the properly executed onset of the classically trained singer, the exact amount of air (neither too much nor too little) passes over the vocal folds; both breathy and pressed phonations are thereby avoided. With silent breath renewal, subglottic pressure returns to the level registered at the initial inspiratory gesture. Precision in the onset technique is scientifically verifiable through studies of airflow and subglottic pressure.[4] This method for uniting airflow and phonation is traditionally known as *l'attacco del suono* (the attack of the sound). It is present in voice-training treatises of the nineteenth century and in most major manuals of the twentieth century. Because the expression "attack the sound" may produce too aggressive glottal activity, many modern-day teachers of singing substitute other language: *the onset of the sound, le commencement du son,* and *der Einsatz.* These terms are psychologically more favorable than *l'attacco.*

Breath management is not improved by attempting to hold the breath for long periods of time, by sustaining isolated long notes and phrases, nor through quick, noisy breath expulsion, but through repetition and extension of the onset–release–breath-renewal maneuver. Nor should the soprano (or any other singer) be advised to expel all the air from her lungs at the close of each phrase: it is not physically possible, and such advice inhibits the instantaneous incorporation of breath renewal into the release.

As mentioned previously, the musculature of the anterolateral abdomen, assisted by muscles of the pectoral region, to a great extent controls the activity of the muscles of the chest wall. The singer remains close to the original inspiratory posture for the execution of each brief onset exercise. By maintaining the position of inspiration, the transverse abdominis, the internal oblique, the external oblique, and, to a lesser extent, the rectus abdominis accomplish the *appoggio;* tonic, dynamic muscle contact permits immediate renewal of the inspiratory gesture.

In extended ranges of the singing voice, because of the stretching, thinning process that produces higher pitches (described in chapter 2), vocal-fold closure during the vibratory cycle is of greater duration than it is in speaking, offering greater resistance to airflow. For that reason, during singing, the inward movement of the epigastric-umbilical region, which is so characteristic of brief bursts of speech, must be delayed, not encouraged.

Balancing the aerodynamic-myoelastic activity of sung phonation is historically known as *la lotta vocale* (*or la lutte vocale* [the vocal contest]) and was described by

Francesco Lamperti around 1860.[5] Such antagonism between the inspiratory and ex-piratory muscle groups is essential to ensure maintenance of a low level of subglot-tic pressure over a longer period of time. Normally, as air passes over the vocal folds in nonphonatory breath cycles, or even in speech, lung volume decreases rapidly and subglottic pressure quickly rises. To combat this expiratory action in order to meet the extended duties of singing, the ribcage must stay well expanded so that the di-aphragm will remain as low as possible for as long as possible (retarded diaphrag-matic ascent; see fig. 4.2). Telling a performer to sing from the diaphragm, to hold the diaphragm down, to push it up, or to control it directly invites confusion. When some established singers speak of "singing from the diaphragm," they can only mean exercising a learned command over the musculature surrounding it, because the diaphragm itself registers no sensation; the singer knows what the diaphragm is doing only from an awareness of abdominal-wall muscle contact, from the observ-able external movement of that region of the body, and from the diminishing and replenishing of breath reserves.

In summary, what is needed for efficient breath management in singing is a sys-tem that ensures an exact amount of airflow commensurate with vocal-fold resist-ance, a coordinated function determined by *tessitura* and intensity levels, and by the requirements of phonetic articulation. Tonal concept and the musicianly ear must be trained to recognize the physical maneuvers that produce the desired vocal sound. Accompanying sensations must be repeated until they become second nature.

However, it is only by establishing a well-defined mental concept of tone that the singer can consistently call upon the activities described above. That tonal concept is acquired by methodically adhering to what becomes the most crucial aspect of the art of singing: *elimination of falsification of vocal timbre by means of acoustic and phys-iologic freedom.*

When physical impediments intrude, free vocal timbre cannot be readily con-ceptualized, regardless of a meritorious tonal intent. For this reason, functional efficiency must be established through technical discipline, as provided by the onset–release–breath-renewal exercises. The *appoggio* approach to breath manage-ment stands in opposition to techniques of "breath support" that control breath exit through induced abdominal-wall movement (inward abdominal thrusting, known as the "in-and-up method"), or, conversely, through outward pushing on the ab-dominal wall (the "down-and-out method," also termed "belly breathing").

The muscle fibers of the abdominal wall have their origins in the pelvic region and insertions in the ribcage, including the lowest back ribs (eleven and twelve), so that muscular expansion is tactually discernible. (See figs. 4.3 and 4.4.) The anatom-ical region for breath management control is best located superficially by placing the fingers at the sides of the torso just under the ribcage and immediately above the hipbone below the tenth rib, with the fingers in light contact with the anterior, lat-eral, and dorsal regions of the abdominal wall. During complete inhalation, with the thumbs placed at the twelfth rib (the costal that defines the base of the ribcage dorsally) and the fingers placed laterally below the frontal tenth rib (bottom of the thoracic cage anteriorly), the singer becomes aware of outward movement of the lowest ribs—both dorsal and anterior—but, more important, of expansion in the lateral abdominal and low dorsal walls of the torso. The systematic onset-release-renewal cycle increases the expansion possibility of these musculatures, which will grow progressively as the exercises are routined.

Having established proper external-frame support of the larynx through the noble posture, the singer takes a complete but silent breath, without any sensation of expansion in the upper chest wall (the pectorals are already in a comfortably elevated position). Inspiration can be accomplished slowly or quickly, through either the nose or the mouth. Tactile awareness of the retention of this contact among muscle groups during a breath cycle is possible even in the absence of phonation. The initial sense of contact felt in the region between the bottom of the ribcage (the tenth rib in front, the eleventh and twelve ribs in back) and the crest of the iliac (hipbone) is maintained. This is the *appoggio* posture.

In the female torso there generally is little space between the tenth rib (the lowest rib in the front of the cage) and the hipbone. This space between the bottom of the thoracic cage and the top of the hipbone may be greater in some females than in others, depending on how compactly they are built. Tenors, and some baritones who have compact cages, often have twice as much space between the bottom of the ribcage and the hipbone as most female singers. Bass-baritones and basses with long torsos generally have less room between the ribcage and the hipbone; their cages are closer to the iliac region than that of the typical tenor or even of the lyric baritone. It is important for teachers of singing, especially men who teach women and women who teach men, to be aware of these structural differences.)

Locating this area of the torso, the singer intones with loosely closed lips a firm "mm-hm!" at a stage-level dynamic, noting the degree of contact the maneuver induces among muscles that intersect the lateral and dorsal walls. Although, as has been seen, the origin of these muscles is in the region of the pelvis, their insertions (fibrous endings) extend upward into the torso as high as the fifth rib, that is, to the origin of the nipple. (See figs. 4.3 and 4.4.) This topographical indicator (the nipple) also reveals the approximate upper location of the central tendon of the diaphragm in its attachment to the pericardium, in which the heart is housed. (The diaphragm is *not* at the level of the navel.)

After establishing good posture, with the hands still in the same position on the torso, the singer repeats, with mouth closed, a series of rapid "hm-hm-hm-hm-hm!" phonations at an easy speech-intonation level, as in intimate laughter. Note that there is no inward pulling of the hypogastric (pubic) abdominal wall nor of the epigastrium (between the navel and the sternum), nor is there any pushing outward in either area. The singer remains in the *appoggio* posture—the inspiratory position—while articulating brief patterns of gentle, laughlike impulses. This natural function of rapid light laughter produces *slight* articulatory motion in the umbilical-abdominal area

EXAMPLE 4.1.

[hm - hm - hm - hm - hm!   -   ]

EXAMPLE 4.2.

[m] —— [m] —— [m] —— [m] —— [m]————

while the singer retains, without tension, the inspiratory posture of the abdominal wall. (Such minimal abdominal movement resembles rapid silent panting or suppressed laughter.)

This leads directly to the first singing exercise for establishing awareness of contact among muscles of the anterolateral abdominal region. With closed lips, the rapid "hm-hm-hm-hm-hm!" series that has just been accomplished at a comfortable speech level is now extended at a moderately quick tempo over an articulated legato 5–4–3–2–1 pattern (ex. 4.1). The individual notes of the 5–4–3–2–1 pattern are next hummed as separate onsets, each of about three second duration (ex. 4.2). After each onset, breath renewal is taken through the nose. This simple exercise develops the freedom to release the glottis and to silently renew the breath. During execution of the 5–4–3–2–1 series of example 4.2, the abdominal wall and the torso remain close to the initial inspiratory position, while the glottis abducts (opens) for each breath renewal and adducts (closes) for each onset of tone, irrespective of tempo. Although there is some awareness of quick, gentle epigastric-abdominal pulsing, the abdominal wall does not move in and out with pitch change; conscious inward thrusting on each onset is to be avoided. Breath renewal comes not from the need to replenish the breath between phonations but because the singer has the freedom to let go at the glottis.

For the duration of each brief exercise, the singer can remain in the inspiratory position without letting the ribcage collapse, without lowering the sternum, and without inward or outward thrusting of the abdominal wall. Inspiration occurs automatically and silently. There is the feeling that one remains in the inspiratory position; breath is replenished without any sensation of stuffing the lungs. "Don't crowd the lungs, only satisfy them," says the Lamperti school.[6] Several minutes should be devoted daily to the hummed onset vocalise of the 5–4–3–2–1 pattern.

EXAMPLE 4.3.

[m - a m - a m - a m - a m - a]

EXAMPLE 4.4.

[ha- ha- ha- ha- ha- ha- ha- ha - ha]
[he - he - he - he - he - he - he - he - he]

The exercise should next be extended by alternating the 5–4–3–2–1 pattern between "humming" and "voweling": [m-a, m-a, m-a, m-a, m-a], with the hum and the vowel each receiving equal duration and intensity (ex. 4.3). During execution of the vowel, the *appoggio* position established for the hum remains. There is no chest displacement. As mentioned above, the only motion is a very small articulatory impulse experienced in the umbilical-abdominal wall.

Onsets with back and front vowels introduced by a lightly and quickly aspirated [h] are sung on a single pitch (ex. 4.4). These patterns may be practiced at varying tempi, beginning moderato. Whether onsets are short or long, the silent breath-renewal process allows the ribcage to remain comfortably expanded without displacement. Although it remains flexible, the abdominal wall does not alter its basic position throughout these exercises. This pattern should be executed in comfortable lower middle and upper middle ranges, alternating lateral (front) and rounded (back) vowels.

An exercise (ex. 4.5) that paces both phonation and breath renewal introduces gradual rhythmic subdivision of the quarter-note onset. The basic onset exercise is now expanded to include single, duplet, triplet, and quadruplet units. The breath is silently renewed while the torso remains in the same position. In the case of the single quarter note and the eighth-note doubles, vocal folds part (abduct) to accommodate the inspiratory gesture following each note, then approximate (adduct) for the next brief phonation. In the triplet pattern, the vocal folds part after each note, but breath is renewed only after the third note. In the quadruplet pattern, the vocal folds part after each note, but breath is renewed only after the fourth note of the gruppetto. To achieve the goal of the exercise, a barely perceptible but completely inaudible breath must be taken *after* the singles, and *between* the duplets, but only *after* each triplet and each quadruplet figure, as marked. This assures that the glottis is being schooled to release (abduct) silently after each rapidly articulated note, independent of breath renewal. The singer thereby develops a high degree of laryngeal freedom. Without

EXAMPLE 4.5.

EXAMPLE 4.6.

displacement of the sternum, the pectoral muscles, or the abdominal wall during either phonation or breath renewal, the entire body remains in a quiet axial position. "Why get out of the position of singing to breathe? Why get out of the position of breathing to sing?" runs another adage of the Lamperti school.

These glottal actions take place below the level of conscious control. A singer should never attempt to open or close her glottis locally, nor to open or close her throat. Onsets should be drilled at first only in a comfortable range of the voice. Single vowels, both lateral and rounded, are used alternately.

Additional exercises for drilling the rhythmic pacing of breath renewal should progress from the short onset patterns to the sustained phrase. A typical sostenuto appendage to the onset series is the 8–9–10–9–8–5–3–5–1 pattern (ex. 4.6). The singer must take care to avoid displacing either the abdominal wall or the upper chest during the sustained phrase. The torso remains *appoggiato*.

This is not to suggest that the inspiratory posture of the torso never alters during a phrase of long duration. During sostenuto, as seconds of phonation go by, the singer does not attempt to remain rigidly in the initial *appoggio* position. As the end of a long phrase approaches, there may be some slight inward motion in the region of the epigastrium, but it is at a rate greatly reduced from that which occurs even in energized speech. However, the sternum and the ribcage neither fall nor collapse during the expiratory gesture or at the conclusion of the phrase. Lateral-dorsal muscle stability tends to remain. As indicated above, during even a sustained exercise there should be almost no chest movement. The *appoggio* technique of breath management ensures retention of this noble position.

In accomplishing the brief onset, the singer has the feeling that breath renewal occurs automatically; it happens of its own accord without any conscious effort to control it. There is no attempt to force expansion of the ribcage, no attempt to fill

EXAMPLE 4.7.

EXAMPLE 4.8.

the lungs. One silently replenishes the breath while remaining in the *appoggio* position, vocal folds abducting for inhalation and adducting for the next onset. There is a perception of openness in the ribcage and in the larynx whether one is singing or breathing, but conscious control lies only in the abdominal wall; the muscles of the abdominal wall remain in antagonistic contact.

Onset exercises should be extended to include ascending and descending patterns on triads and arpeggios, as in examples 4.7 and 4.8. The singer may wish to use a single vowel or to change the vowel sequence as the rhythmic pattern alters. It is advisable to employ all of the cardinal vowels. As suggested by the commentary regarding these series of exercises, executing the onset maneuver in varying rhythmic pacings is crucial to developing breath management for more expansive singing tasks. The rapid onset is related to staccato passages, examples of which are readily found in the vocal literature, particularly that of the coloratura soprano. In quickly moving staccato singing, the vocal folds must engage and disengage rapidly (independent of breath renewal). For that reason, the staccato maneuver is identical to those in all other forms of onset; however, it is not a pedagogic substitute for the basic onset procedure.

These patterns are to be practiced sequentially throughout neighboring keys. Vocal-fold adduction for the commencement of each note should be accomplished by two modes of onset:

1. Normally with a lightly aspirated [h] (even in the aspirated onset, audible expulsion of breath is always to be averted), during which a minuscule amount of airflow introduces the subsequent vowel.

2. Occasionally with a barely perceptible stroke of the glottis, with no airflow
   in advance of the onset of the sound. (A heavy *coup de glotte* [hard glottal
   closure] is always to be avoided.)

The release (the parting of the vocal folds, sometimes termed the *offset*) is just as
precise as the meeting of the vocal folds (*onset*). The new breath, it should be reiterated, is instantaneous with the release: adduction–abduction–silent breath renewal.

Although the speed with which these exercises are to be drilled depends somewhat
on the size and category of the soprano voice, a metronome marking of 60 to ♩ is
an appropriate tempo for most female singers. More dramatic voices may wish to
sustain each note longer than the indicated metronome marking.

In the literature itself we find composers making use of interjected onsets for both
vocal display and emotion. In his *"Blessed Virgin's Expostulation"* (*Harmonia Sacra*,
here in transposition for soprano voice), Purcell combines brief onsets with subsequent melismatic passages (ex. 4.9). This alternation of onset and agility intentionally
produces a questing character that masterfully catches the Virgin's disquietude. Breath
renewal following each brief utterance must be silent. The singer feels she need only
replenish the small amount of breath she has used. In actuality, the entire respiratory tidal volume is replenished.

For purposes of heightened expression, as in *"Als Luise die Briefe ihres ungetreuen
Liebhabers verbrannte,"* Mozart also depends on brief, detached onsets (ex. 4.10).
A passage such as "Ihr brennet nun, und bald, ihr Lieben, ist keine Spur von euch
mehr hier" could have been composed in such a way that the singer would deliver
the entire phrase in one breath. By breaking up the phrase into small units, Mozart
heightens the emotion. In so doing, he mirrors the onset-release exercises of historic
voice pedagogy. Silent breath renewal takes place, each release being as distinctly
marked as each onset.

Examples 4.9 and 4.10 are suitable to sopranos of all vocal weight. These patterns
should be practiced sequentially through several tonalities.

In the opening vocal passage of the frequently excerpted *Roméo et Juliette* (Gounod)
waltz, Juliette's exuberance is expressed through brief interjectory phonations. This

EXAMPLE 4.9.

EXAMPLE 4.10.

und all die schwär - me - ri - schen Lie - der, denn ach!　er sang nicht mir al -

lein.　Ihr bren - net nun, und　bald, ihr Lie - ben, ist kei - ne　Spur von euch mehr hier.

EXAMPLE 4.11.

Je　　veux　　vi - vre - dans　le　　rê - ve -

qui　m'en - i - vre　Ce - jour - en - cor!

passage from "*Je veux vivre*" (ex. 4.11) serves admirably as an exercise in rapid silent replenishment of the breath while the singer remains in the *appoggio* posture. Transposed through several keys as a vocalise for soprano voices of light category, it can be a valuable daily onset-release and silent-breath-renewal drill. The admonition regarding clean onset and release suggested for examples 4.9 and 4.10 pertains here as well.

Because of the speechlike inflection, it is often in the recitative portion of the operatic *scena* that the singer best routines clean onset and efficient renewal of the breath; they become of special importance for the later sostenuto sections of the aria. For the dramatic soprano voice, and for purposes of the drama itself, the recitative "Abscheulicher! wo eilst du hin? was hast du vor? was hast du vor in wildem Grimme?" (*Fidelio*, Beethoven) supplies for the dramatic soprano voice several onset–breath-management passages similar in technical construction to the examples cited thus far. Beethoven uses the same compositional device in the opening phrases of lyric-soprano Marzelline's aria (*Fidelio*) "*O wär ich schon mit dir vereint*" (see ex. 4.13). In fact, in much of his vocal writing Beethoven employs rapid interjections—emotive use of onsets and pacing of the breath—followed by sustained passages; consider Florestan's aria (*Fidelio*) and the writing for the solo voices in the Ninth Symphony.

In composing for the soprano voice, Bellini ingeniously accesses deep emotion through series of phrases that pace alternating onset and quiet breath renewal. The

EXAMPLE 4.12.

Rezitativ

Ab - scheu - li-cher!   wo eilst du hin?   was hast du vor?

was hast du vor in wil - dem Grim - me?

EXAMPLE 4.13.

O wär' ich schon mit dir___ ver-eint und dürf - te Mann dich

nen - nen! Ein Mäd - chen darf ja, was es meint, zur Hälf - te nur be - ken - nen!

recitativo accompagnato passage beginning "Eccomi in lieta vesta" that introduces the aria "*Oh! quante volte*" (*I Capuleti e i Montecchi*) is a superb study in the dramatic alternation of sound and silence (ex. 4.14). Additionally, the juxtaposition of brief middle-voice phrases with melismatic flight into upper voice makes this recitative a valuable vehicle for adjusting breath energy in mounting phrases, a topic that will receive more attention in chapter 10. Rhythmic exactitude should be maintained throughout "siate, ah! siate per me faci ferali," with no liberty taken beyond that indicated by each fermata. (This is not the occasion for disjunct rubato.) The ample recitative ought to be memorized by sopranos of every category for use as part of the daily technical routine.

Verdi, in Gilda's opening phrases (ex. 4.15) from "*Caro nome*" (*Rigoletto*), expresses romantic ecstasy through sequential onsets similar to others considered here. The detached syllables must not be treated in semistaccato fashion, but given their full rhythmic value. There should be no decrescendo toward the termination of each syllable, but rather dynamic constancy. Otherwise, the passage becomes flip rather than rapturous, and the essential forward phrase movement is negated.

Clearly, in this passage and in the other cited examples, as well as in those that follow, the broken syllables and brief groupings of words (small units within an overall phrase) could be vocally accomplished without the composer's written-in intervening pauses and breath renewals between syllables or words. The brief interjectory silences found in the cited passages attest that major composers understood how the

EXAMPLE 4.14.

Ec - co - mi in lie - ta ve - sta... Ec - comi a - dor - na... come vit - ti - ma all'a - ra.

Oh! al - men po - tes - si qual vit - ti - ma ca - der del - l'a - ra al pie - de!

O nu - zi - a - li te - de ab - bor - ri - te co - sì, co - sì, fa - ta - li,

siate, ah! sia - te per me fa - ci fe -

ra - li.

EXAMPLE 4.15.

Ca - ro no - me che il mio cor fe - sti pri - mo pal - pi -

tar, le de - li - zie del - l'a - mor mi dei sem - pre ram - men - tar!

technical maneuvers of voice production could be put to use in the enhancement of dramatic expression. The mode of composition takes into account the inherent expressive possibilities of finely honed prephonatory tuning (conceptualizing the sound in advance of its initiation) of the *appoggio* onset–release–breath-renewal procedure. Pitch targeting is immediate and accurate because onset and release are incorporated into the total phrase shape.

In the passage from "*Caro nome*" discussed earlier, renewal of the breath is so immediate that it seems imperceptible even to the singer herself. She maintains a feeling of openness (induced by the inspiratory gesture) during both silence and song, whether or not actual breath renewal takes place during the brief interpolations of silence. The abdominal wall and the chest remain in one position. It is characteristic

EXAMPLE 4.16.

of these onsets interjected into textual and musical phrases, whether in Purcell, Mozart, Bellini, Gounod, or Verdi, that they do not interrupt forward phrase movement but assist it. The clean onsets and releases propel phrase direction; inefficient, audible breath renewal hinders phrase movement.

For a technically advanced and well-established voice of large dimension, the *cabaletta* portion of "*Non mi dir*" (*Don Giovanni*, Mozart) combines repeated onsets with pyrotechnical melismatic display (ex. 4.16). The singer may transpose the original passage to a lower key, then progress upward through several neighboring keys. In traditional performance practice, onset-release and breath renewal follow the passage as edited in example 4.16. Is it necessary to renew the breath after the staccato $B\flat_5$ and $A\flat_5$ (high B$\flat$ and high A), or is it sufficient for the clean release and onset to occur independently of breath renewal? The answer will depend on the singer's individual preference—on how comfortable she is executing the liberating device of

EXAMPLE 4.17.

quick breath renewal adapted from the short onset exercises. Certainly, if she tries to crowd the lungs (rather than follow the easy breath replenishment procedure of the *appoggio*), she will do better to disregard the inserted inhalatory indications. However, by letting go at the glottis while retaining the feeling that she is simply renewing the minimal amount of breath she has just used, the soprano will reduce a tendency to accumulate tension that the passage might otherwise induce, and at the same time she will accomplish the emotional intent of the passage.

Nor is the onset as an emotive device foreign to the Verdian opera *scena* form. Although the entire aria should be undertaken only by a sizable and technically secure voice, the opening phrases of "Ah fors' è lui" (*La traviata*), particularly when transposed sequentially, can serve all categories of soprano as an advantageous exercise in combining vocal onset and relatively brief subsequent phrases (see ex. 4.17). It is not assumed here that the breath will be renewed throughout the cavatina at each sixteenth-note interruption of the line in "Ah fors' è lui" and "godea sovente" (or in comparable moments, depending on adherence to traditional cuts). But the quick engagement and disengagement of the vocal folds on the short notes resembles the onset-release action experienced in the triplet and quadruplet figures of examples 4.5 and 4.7, in which the vocal folds swing open independently of breath renewal. Such freedom of vocal-fold action permits the breath to be taken selectively, as frequently as desired, without any perceived interruption of phonation.

Again Verdi, in Leonora's dramatic *cabaletta* from "*Tacea la notte*" (*Il trovatore*), with its alternation of detached or staccato notes and connected brief notes, offers a remarkable passage in rapid, precise onset, agility, and breath-renewal sequences (ex. 4.18). The soprano with a voice of ample dimensions should memorize this excerpt for use as a formula for breath-management calisthenics; it provides a valuable vocalization vehicle for the large, mature lyric or spinto voice that already possesses a high level of skill.

Twentieth-century composers have not lost interest in the potential for musical and emotional expression through the disjunct phrase and the repeated vocal onset. A typical example (ex. 4.19) comes from Milton Babbitt's "*Sounds and Words*".

EXAMPLE 4.18.

d'a-mor, che in-ten - do io so - la, il cor, il

cor, il cor, s'in -ne - bri - ò. Mo - ri -

rò, ah, si, per es - so mo - ri - rò, per es-so mo-ri -

rò, mo - ri - rò,

EXAMPLE 4.19.

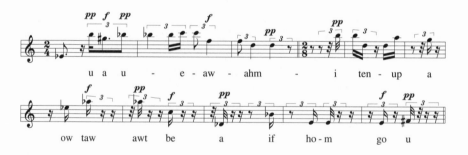

u a u - e - aw - ahm - i ten - up a

ow taw awt be a if ho - m go u

Rapid silent breath renewal and clean onset are as essential to this idiom as to its predecessors. Good breath-management techniques bridge styles and time periods. The singer and the teacher are encouraged to use the performance literature to supplement basic onset exercises. Both types of material offer precision exercises that efficiently coordinate airflow and vocal-fold approximation. They contribute to technical prowess and vowel health and thus form part of the daily routine of every serious singer, regardless of *Fach*.

However, it would be a mistake to think that *appoggio* concerns only breath management. Many times when a singer feels that "support" is lacking, the technical problem may lie in laryngeal or resonator-tract tensions. *Appoggio* is not just a matter of breath control but of the uniting of motor, vibrator, and resonator activity into one whole. The *appoggio* results from the synergy of aerodynamic, laryngeal, and supraglottic action. For example, if the larynx is elevated or depressed as part of voice production, or if the external frame support of the neck (*appoggio della nucca*) is not operative, the laryngeal response to airflow will be defective. A sung phonation may sound "unsupported," leading the singer to think that the problem is one of breath management. Additional encounters with the technical aspects of breath management as related to sostenuto and to vocal registration will be discussed in chapters 9 and 10.

The soubrette, the soubrette/coloratura, and the lyric soprano will wish to take the onset exercises and the excerpted literature passages into higher keys than will a more dramatic voice. They ought to avoid passages that have been marked as vocalization material for heavier soprano voices. Although some of the passages are equally adaptable for all sopranos, in keeping with the realization that *Fach* subdivisions exist within the general soprano category, the spinto and the dramatic should not be expected to use the same tonalities as do the lighter instruments for executing the exercises.

5

The Agility Factor

No matter how sizable or dramatic a soprano instrument, it needs to flexibly perform rapid movement. If a singer is unable to freely move the voice in swift melismas, there will be a corresponding lack of freedom in slow, sustained passages.

However, the soubrette, the coloratura, and the lyric soprano generally tend to move ahead more quickly in gaining agility than the dramatic soprano. The lirico spinto, the dramatic, and the *Zwischenfachsängerin* should spend considerable time on basic agility exercises and when first working on them should not expect to execute the patterns as rapidly as do lighter voices. Many sopranos with large voices feel as though their instruments are unwieldy in quickly moving passages; this is perfectly normal. With patience and fortitude, the larger soprano voice will be able to acquire agility skill equal to that of the lyric.

The two poles of bel canto writing for soprano voices of all size and weight are the cavatina and the cabaletta of the classic opera scena. Most soprano arias by Mozart, Rossini, Bellini, Donizetti, and their contemporaries, and even those by Verdi, are based on the two contrasting segments of the scena: sostenuto and movement. Handel and composers of the Neapolitan school, who mostly used the da capo (ABA) rather than the scena form, also require remarkable contrasts between moments of quietude and those of motion. For the accomplished soprano of any *Fach,* much of the standard vocal literature is a testing ground for the exhibition of sostenuto and velocity skills.

A basic premise of this book is that a reliable vocal technique is best acquired by progressively treating identifiable vocal tasks in a systematic way. In natural sequence, the study of velocity evolves directly from the onset. After clean onset, release, and quiet breath renewal have become relatively secure, agility should be the next technical facet to be addressed. In the vocal literature itself, it is almost impossible to separate onset and agility assignments—witness a number of the literature passages cited in the previous chapter.

EXAMPLE 5.1.

EXAMPLE 5.2.

Having acquired skill in the onset and developed an understanding of *appoggio* breath management, the singer next turns to rapid staccato passages built on triads (ex. 5.1). For most sopranos these figures commence in upper middle voice and move upward by semitone, progressing sequentially from the key of A through that of D, thereafter descending through the keys of D♭, C, B, B♭ and A, to A♭. (It is well to return to a tonality slightly below that in which the vocalise began.)

In the subsequent exercises, the choice of vowel should be constantly varied. A vocalise may be sung on a series of single vowels, or vowels may shift within the same exercise. Front, mixed, and back vowels should all be used. The same process is extended to arpeggiated figures (ex. 5.2) beginning in the tonality of F, progressing through that of A, and descending to the key of E. Dramatic voices may wish to begin a semitone or whole tone lower.

As represented in the melismatic writing (*melismata*) of traditional solo vocal literature, velocity skill comes in two forms: staccato, and articulated legato. With regard to breath management, the articulated legato passage is executed in the same technical manner as the staccato passage; the two modes differ only in that the notes of the first are detached and those of the second connected. Although the extent of discernible epigastric-umbilical movement varies with the degree of articulation desired, physical activity remains about the same for both modes.

Staccato and articulated legato resemble the abdominal action found in subtle laughter (especially of the suppressed sort) and in panting (particularly silent panting). A good way to experience the proper implementation of staccato facility is to begin with onsets of easy low-voiced laughter, as encountered earlier in example 4.1. This procedure is then distributed over longer patterns built on both small and large intervals.

First, consideration of the staccato mode.

As seen in chapter 4, rapid engagement and disengagement of the vocal folds take place when silent breath renewal is interposed between detached pitches. The same

EXAMPLE 5.3.

engagement-disengagement of the vocal folds and breath replenishment occur in staccato, sung at moderate tempo. But rapid *gruppetti* are articulated in staccato mode, with breath renewal occurring only at phrase endings (ex. 5.3). This activity is generated by small impulses in the umbilical-epigastric wall that activate the exact amount of breath energy required for the indicated pitches. As with this entire series of vocalises, the exercise should be sung in a variety of keys.

In the literature, a problem frequently surfaces in the execution of quick staccato passages, because in contrast to the natural articulatory movements of rapid silent panting or suppressed laughter, the singer progressively pulls inward on the abdominal wall. On the contrary, there should be no more conscious inward motion in the lateral-anterior abdominal wall during the execution of a staccato (or articulated legato) passage than occurs in normal gentle laughter, where inward thrusting is minimal or nonexistent.

To be avoided is the conjecture that vibrato must be removed from velocity patterns just because each note of the melisma cannot accommodate the same number of vibrato excursions per second as the long notes of a sostenuto passage. The error lies in the supposition that vibrato is perceived by the listening ear as a pitch variant rather than as a timbre component. In actuality, in vibrato excursion both frequency and pitch variants are distributed over the duration of an entire velocity passage and are not bound to an equal number of completed cycles per second on each note of the melisma. Performing velocity passages with straight-tone timbre reduces airflow efficiency and causes a loss in consistency of vocal timbre. Straight-toning should never be the result of an inability to maintain a free vocal production during the execution of rapidly moving figures.

Yet another device to be shunned is the aspirated melisma, that is, the insertion of an audible [h] before each note of a running pattern. This results in the "Ha-ha-ha-ha!" school of articulation, to the detriment of timbre and style. Reliance on constant "ha-ha-ha-ha"-ing in order to manage pyrotechnical agility has no place in schooled solo singing. Increasing the rate of airflow as a means of melismatic articulation becomes highly mannered and aesthetically displeasing.

Perhaps the choral conductor, as a desperation solution for large ensembles whose singers are largely amateurs, may be forgiven for an occasional use of aspirated articulation. However, the disastrous effects on choral tone caused by constant aspirated articulation will be reduced if the choristers restrict such aspiration to the first

EXAMPLE 5.4.

EXAMPLE 5.5.

note of each sixteenth-note *gruppetto* (or to the first sixteenth of two *gruppetti*). This provides points of rhythmic exactitude not possible when escaping air occurs after each note of a *gruppetto*. When not relied on excessively, some limited aspiration for rhythmic accentuation on important notes in extensive melismas can be useful to the solo singer as well. But making a habit of this practice is to be avoided.

The soprano should continue staccato work by choosing a pattern based on the interval of a second (ex. 5.4). It is evident that this staccato exercise grows organically out of the onset series. Beginning for most sopranos in the key of A, the exercise should be extended into upper middle voice.

Now to the articulated legato mode.

Example 5.4 should be expanded to include alternating bars of staccato and articulated legato (ex. 5.5). Gentle impulsing in the abdominal region (not a movement of continuous inward thrusts) facilitates maintenance of the staccato activity in the subsequent legato mode but without vocal-fold abduction after each note (that is, during the second measure of the exercise). The important thing is that the legato portion be accomplished with the identical minimal pulsing of the umbilical-epigastric movement that occurs when executing the staccato portion (though it is less marked in articulated legato). Regardless of the rapidity of either the staccato or the legato mode, equal vibrancy must prevail. Example 5.5 should be sung in a number of middle-voice tonalities.

Subsequently, short patterns that alternate staccato and legato may be introduced. These brief patterns are best sung first on ascending passing-tone patterns within intervals of thirds, fourths and fifths using both lateral and rounded vowels (ex. 5.6, 5.7, and 5.8). At the same time that legato-staccato articulation is routined, *appoggio* technique is being reinforced. Then pitch direction is reversed (ex. 5.9, 5.10, and 5.11).

Example 5.12 illustrates how cardinal vowels may be used in various combinations to alternate staccato and articulated legato modes. Thereafter, both ascending and descending pitch directions (ex. 5.13) should be united in a single phrase of articulated

EXAMPLE 5.6.

EXAMPLE 5.7.

EXAMPLE 5.8.

EXAMPLE 5.9.

EXAMPLE 5.10.

EXAMPLE 5.11.

EXAMPLE 5.12.

[i]   [e]   [ɑ]   [o]   [u]

EXAMPLE 5.13.

EXAMPLE 5.14.

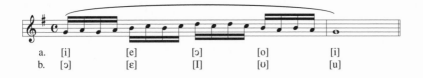

EXAMPLE 5.15.

legato, alternating lateral and rounded vowels. (Vowel combinations other than those illustrated in ex. 5.13 may be substituted.) The exercise is sung at a rapid pace (more quickly by the soubrette than by the dramatic) in several keys in middle range.

Composers often request unexpected melismatic turns, especially from sopranos. Example 5.14 presents unanticipated changes of direction. The rapid pattern can be moved into upper range. Single vowels and the combinations indicated in (a) and (b) are suggested. Numerous examples of similar melismatic twists can be located in the performance literature.

A long-standing favorite agility exercise in many voice studios is the five-note–nine-note ascending and descending scale of example 5.15. It ought to be sung on a series of single vowels in several neighboring keys.

Rapid passages built on seventh-chord progressions (major, minor, and diminished), as in example 5.16, alert the singer to vowel integrity, clean articulation, and intonation precision in quickly changing patterns. These figures should be sung consecutively in several neighboring tonalities.

Regulation of the degrees of breath energy needed for rapidly occurring agility patterns that extend from lower to upper ranges may be routined through example 5.17.

Example 5.16.

Example 5.17.

Example 5.18.

This vocalise begins by using the legato abdominal-wall articulation encountered earlier in example 5.4. There follows a rapid scalar ascent, with the interval of a second in example 5.4 now executed with increased energy in transposition to the upper octave. Then the melisma rapidly descends to the lower octave to repeat the original pattern of example 5.4. The initial umbilical-epigastric pulsing becomes more marked at the upper octave. Energy is readjusted for the descending scale and for the concluding articulated seconds, which alternate staccato and articulated-legato modes. This is an advanced exercise in rapid articulation and must be reserved to the singer who already has the *appoggio* technique well in hand.

Another challenging agility exercise (ex. 5.18) consists of close intervals descending and ascending in triplets and in quadruplets. It should be undertaken only after the shorter, less complex exercises have been mastered.

EXAMPLE 5.19.

EXAMPLE 5.20.

The literature for all categories of soprano voice is rich in agility passages that can form part of soprano velocity-skill training. Nothing better could be devised as an agility challenge (especially for the soubrette and the coloratura) than Handel's "*Oh Had I Jubal's Lyre.*" The passage beginning "in songs like hers" leads into an extensive melisma (ex. 5.19) on the second syllable of the word "rejoice," which takes unexpected turns of direction.

Equally beneficial are the familiar *Messiah* "rejoice" passages (ex. 5.20), with their irregular *gruppetti* that so often plague a soprano whose vocal endowment must be sufficiently sumptuous to later bring impressive sostenuto skill to "*I Know that My Redeemer Liveth.*" Handel, a composer who offers singers lessons in all aspects of voice technique (exceeded only by Mozart), frequently has his melismas take unexpected directional turns. The soprano who is thoroughly disciplined for such precarious velocity passages is prepared for most future melismatic eventualities. These patterns should be memorized and drilled daily so that they may serve as road maps over similarly bumpy melismatic terrain in songs and arias.

Example 5.21.

Especially for voices of light category, the beloved "*Alleluia*" from the *Exultate, Jubilate* (Mozart) offers grateful instruction in agility (ex. 5.21). As has been suggested, such passages may be sung sequentially, beginning in lower keys, then progressing upward by semitone. Mozart expects melismatic facility from all sopranos, not just those with light instruments. The arpeggiated figures requested of Fiordiligi in "*Come scoglio*" (*Così fan tutte*) provide the ample soprano voice with agility exercises that can serve well as part of the regular warm-up.

Donizetti's works are replete with pyrotechnical melismas for the soprano voice, exemplified in passages from Adina's *L'elisir d'amore* aria "*Prendi.*" Velocity patterns beginning with the text "saggio, onesto, ah! sempre scontento e mesto, no, non sarai così, ah no, non sarai così" and continuing onward through the two-octave melisma on the final syllable of the word *sarai* are perfectly suited as a technical excerpt for the light soprano instrument.

The same composer's ever popular "*So anch'io la virtù magica*" (*Don Pasquale*) provides the soubrette/coloratura and the light lyric soprano a number of lively exercises for rapid execution. Introduced by the text "brillare mi piace scherzar," an extended melismatic pattern on "*ah!*" proffers directional turns, ascending and descending scale passages, and arpeggiation for a dash of charming vocal acrobatics. After the vocalise has been memorized, it can be started at lower pitch, gradually arriving at the G♭ original through a series of progressive half-step tonalities. Because of its brevity and its gracious melismatic flow, the passage should be incorporated as a friendly workout in the soubrette/coloratura's daily routine.

From Bellini's exquisite bel canto aria "*Oh quante volte!*" (*I Capuleti e i Montecchi*) come passages that serve lyric voices as superb exercises for drilling alternating legato

EXAMPLE 5.22.

and melismatic proficiency. The entire final page of music, beginning at "Raggio del tuo sembiante," moves into beautiful melismatic passages at "ah! parmi il brillar del giorno" and "mi sembra un tuo sospir." Such extended passages should first be dealt with in brief repeated segments, then reunited as an entity.

The role of Lucia (*Lucia di Lammermoor*, Donizetti) offers dramatic-coloratura supranos pyrotechnical challenges to satisfy the most ambitious. The dramatic coloratura is as much in need of the ability to move the voice as is her soubrette/coloratura colleague. Even if the entire role of Lucia does not come into question as a performance vehicle, soubrette, coloratura, dramatic-coloratura, and lyric sopranos can profit from the successful negotiation of repeated melismatic patterns, as in "il ciel per me si schiuda" (from "*Regnava nel silenzio*").

In "*Nun eilt herbei!*" (*Die lustigen Weiber von Windsor*, Nicolai), Frau Fluth engages in joyous melismatic sport (ex. 5.22). The juxtaposition of short and long segments in the *cadenza a piacere* makes it especially practical as an exercise in pacing breath management and velocity. It should be sung at varying tempi with both accelerandi and rubati shaping the long melisma. This pattern provides a brief flight of agility to memorize and incorporate into the daily workout as a transposable vocalise for all categories of soprano.

Not only in "*Casta diva*" must Norma (*Norma*, Bellini) display vocal prowess. Throughout the role she is called upon to exhibit highly developed velocity, as in her duet with Adalgisa, beginning with "Pei tuoi" and extending through "fellon, per me." (Mezzo-soprano Adalgisa echoes the high-lying soprano melismatic passages exactly.)

The coloratura soprano will find an excellent exemplar (ex. 5.23) of melismatic requirement for her vocal category in "*Je suis Titania*" (*Mignon*, Thomas). The sequential patterns with their sudden changes of direction are beautifully designed for managing melismatic facility.

Verdi's Violetta (*La traviata*) demands both sustained dramatic singing and climactic agility. Some sopranos find one aspect of the role more comfortable than the other. This is especially true when a coloratura is wrongly cast as Violetta. The

EXAMPLE 5.23.

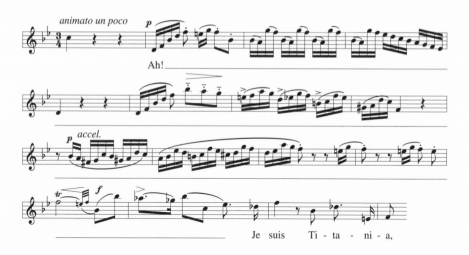

EXAMPLE 5.24.

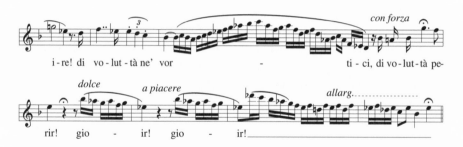

role of Violetta should be sung by a big lyric soprano voice with the melismatic expertise that Verdi clearly intended. There are no better agility exercises for the mature, technically secure, and skilled soprano than the exciting velocity passages from "*Sempre libera*," beginning with "di voluttà ne' vortici" and concluding with the "gioir!" pair, quoted in example 5.24. These passages should first be transposed to lower tonalities, then sung in the original key with such frequency that they become "sung into the voice." They will eventually become as old hat as though performed on "automatic pilot."

Equally suited to the large lyric soprano voice for the development of melismatic capabilities is Rosalinda's *czardas* (*Die Fledermaus*, J. Strauss). The complete aria is a radiant example of the skillful blending of sostenuto and velocity.

With the cabaletta section ("I go to him") of Anne Truelove's "*No Word from Tom*" (*The Rake's Progress*), Stravinsky, in his twentieth-century reincarnation of the eighteenth-century *scena*, produces a potent agility vehicle for the sizable lyric soprano voice. The entire cabaletta is perfectly written for the soprano who must combine dramatic and melismatic facility.

These operatic excerpts, varied to cover most vocal rapidity contingencies for all vocal categories, are to be restricted to advanced singers. Portions consisting of either a few bars or an entire passage serve as technique-schooling devices. The soprano who regularly practices such passages will have a source on which to draw for all foreseeable circumstances.

If a stabilized technique of velocity is the aim, a mix of brief and extended melismas, together with selected passages from the literature, should be part of the daily vocal regimen for both the serious debutante and the established artist. Through techniques of onset and agility, the singer develops both the musculature and the kinesthetic coordination needed to undertake the other singing tasks that lie ahead in a systematic consideration of vocal technique, including the ability to sustain the voice. (Related melismatic material that moves into the flageolet range will be considered in chapter 10.)

6

Resonance in Soprano Voices

Supraglottic Considerations

WHEREAS RESONANCE GOALS AMONG POP AND ETHNIC VOCAL IDIOMS ARE widely divergent, there are common resonance expectations for the classical singer. For the professional musician, "classical" refers to music composed in the late eighteenth century; in lay parlance, classical designates non-pop idioms such as opera, oratorio, lieder, mélodie, and the art song. Here the more general usage pertains. The classical singer is expected to exhibit an evenly modulated scale with good resonance balance, based on the relationship of the fundamental to its generated harmonic partials (overtones).

A complex tone consists of the fundamental and a series of overtones (upper partials). The vocal instrument is rich in such resonance potentials, with a number of harmonic partials available to it. The frequency of each harmonic partial is a multiple of the fundamental frequency. The listener perceives the fundamental (technically the first harmonic) as the sung pitch, but the quality of the sound is dependent on relationships among the partials.

The horizontal axis of a vowel sequence [i–e–a–o–u], sung by a twenty-two-year-old potential lyric soprano (fig. 6.1), represents time, zero to eight seconds; the vertical axis represents frequency, zero to 4000 Hz. A third factor is acoustic energy, represented on the graph by degrees of density: the darker, the higher the concentration of energy.

It can be seen that acoustic response is not limited to the fundamental frequency that is perceived by the listener as the pitch being sung; the evenly spaced horizontal lines (harmonic partials or overtones) are exact multiples of the fundamental frequency. The upper lines of the graph display harmonic partials that determine characteristics of the sound (vowel definition and overall voice timbre).

Regions of strong acoustic response are known as formants. The function of one formant does not negate the influence of others; they complement each other. The balance among formants determines the quality of sung tone. The first formant lies above the fundamental (bottom portion of the spectrum) and yields the "depth" of the voice. The more central second formant largely defines the vowel, and the third

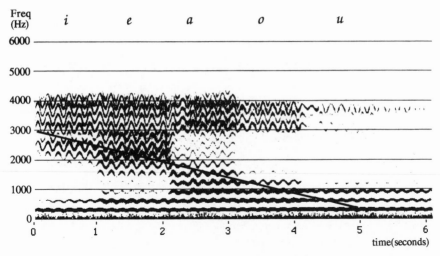

FIGURE 6.1. *Spectrogram of a 22-year-old potential lyric soprano singing an [i–e–a–o–u] sequence on E♭₄. The lower horizontal axis of the graph represents time; the left-hand axis represents frequency in Hz. The first formant is seen at the bottom of the graph; the diagonal line beginning at the left in the middle of the graph (diagonal vowel sequential) shows stepwise descent of the second formant, which attests vowel definition; the third formant occupies the upper regions of the graph, with acoustic strength registered between 3,000 and 4,000 Hz. The wavy lines of the harmonic partials indicate vibrato. (Otto B. Schoepfle Vocal Arts Center, Oberlin Conservatory of Music, 1994)*

formant, which lodges in the upper portion of the spectrum, furnishes the ring, the "focus." Vowel definition produces a downward steplike spectrographic progression (indicated by the horizontal line superimposed on the spectrogram of fig. 6.1) known as the diagonal vowel sequence, moving from approximately 3000 Hz on the vowel [i] to around 800Hz on the vowel [u].

The undulations (waviness) of the partials in the voice spectra indicate the extent of vibrato phenomena. Parameters of the vibrato are

1. the extent of pitch variation,
2. the number of cycles per second, and
3. the timbre results.

By isolating one second of the phonation, the number of vibrato excursions per second can be determined. The phonation of figure 6.1 displays a steady vibrato rate of slightly more than six cycles per second, with a normal rate of pitch excursion.

The spectrography of figure 6.1 shows that this soprano has sufficient technique to distribute acoustic energy within appropriate regions of the spectrum, resulting in efficient sound: there is little or no acoustic activity between the partials, indicating that she has avoided by-noises (harmonics that are not multiples of the fundamental).

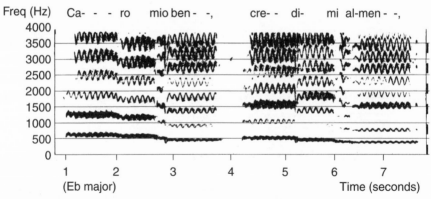

FIGURE 6.2. *Spectrogram of a mature lirico spinto soprano singing "Caro mio ben, credimi almen." The lower horizontal axis of the graph represents time; the left-hand axis represents frequency in Hz. The first formant is seen at the bottom of the graph; the middle of the graph shows the second formant, which attests in vowel definition; the third formant occupies the upper regions of the graph with acoustic strength registered between 2500 and 4000 Hz. Wavy lines of the harmonic partials indicate vibrato. (Otto B. Schoepfle Vocal Arts Center, Oberlin Conservatory of Music, 1995)*

The same phenomena can be observed in the spectrographic display from a mature professional spinto soprano singing "Caro mio ben, credimi almen" in the key of E$^\flat$ (see fig. 6.2).

Resonance balancing characteristically gives the professional voice a completeness of timbre (*voce completa*) through all its ranges. In the historic international school, this desirable quality is known as the chiaroscuro (light-dark) tone, and is uniformly displayed by premier singers trained in classical voice technique. Figure 6.3 shows spectrum analysis superimposed on video performances of two great American sopranos, Eleanor Steber and Leontyne Price. Although the settings of the spectrograms are differently calibrated, the graphs reveal that both sopranos exhibit vibrant, clean singing (no noise elements between essential formants), with upper and lower harmonics in balance with the fundamental. Steber and Price also display

FIGURE 6.3. *Upper figure: spectrogram analysis superimposed on a video performance (Firestone Hour) of soprano Eleanor Steber singing a phrase from the aria "Vissi d'arte" (Tosca, Puccini) "rimuneri così." Steber is pictured singing the [i] vowel in così. The first formant is shown at the bottom of the graph, just above the fundamental; the middle of the graph indicates the second formant, representing vowel definition; the third formant occupies the upper regions of the graph, with acoustic strength registered between 3000 and 4000 Hz. The upper-left window displays a power-spectrum analysis of the same phonation; the upper-right window registers the waveform of the phonation. Wavy lines of the harmonic partials indicate vibrato.*

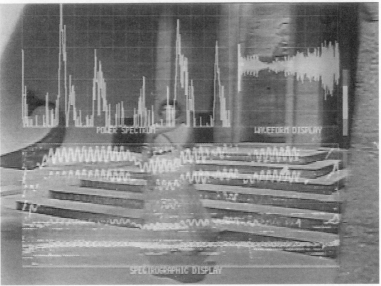

Lower figure: spectrogram analysis superimposed on a video performance (Firestone Hour) of soprano Leontyne Price singing a phrase from the aria "O patria mia" (Aïda, Verdi): "Ah, mai più, mai più!" The first formant is shown at the bottom of the graph, just above the fundamental; the middle of the graph indicates the second formant, which attests vowel definition; the third formant occupies the upper regions of the graph, with acoustic strength registered between 3000 and 4000 Hz. The upper-left window displays a power-spectrum analysis of the same phonation; the upper-right window registers the waveform of the phonation. Wavy lines of the harmonic partials indicate vibrato. (Otto B. Schoepfle Vocal Arts Center, Oberlin Conservatory of Music, 1998)

traditional vibrato rates and the spectral termination in the area of 4000 Hz typical of balanced classical vocalism. Two outstanding Italian sopranos (Renata Tebaldi and Mirella Freni) present harmonic balancing (chiaroscuro) that parallels that of their American-trained colleagues (see fig. 6.4).

By contrast, singers of popular idioms usually make other kinds of choices in overtone combinations, showing harmonic partials several thousand Hz beyond the spectral ceiling typical of the classically trained singer. Much of this acoustic strength represents nonintegers of the fundamental. The upper and lower windows of figure 6.5 represent the spectra of Ethel Merman, an accomplished "belter," who used chest voice in extended range. The performance is mostly without vibrato.

Many exercises from nineteenth-century voice pedagogy manuals are devoted to the chiaroscuro balance. Modern spectral analysis verifies the validity of the age-old pedagogic assumption that beautiful singing should result in timbre characterized by components that are "light and dark," that have "height and depth," "brilliance and warmth," "ping and velvet," and "ring and richness."

Bony and cartilaginous structures of the body, largely those of the torso and the head, serve as conductors of sympathetic vibration. In certain ranges of the vocal scale, when proper balances exist among the laryngeal, pharyngeal and buccal resonators (see fig. 2.1), sympathetic vibration produces empirical sensations in the bony structures of the head. In the historic Italian school, these sensations were termed *l'impostazione della voce*. When the sound felt "placed" in the head, it was considered to be *imposto*. Much of the subjective language about resonation that lingers on in voice pedagogy is an attempt to describe the sensation of *l'impostazione della voce*. In point of fact, it is only with specificity of language, and by the modeling of sound, that *l'imposto* can be conveyed.

Some females have little awareness of a change in vibratory sensation when moving from one part of the range to another. But for most, in the lowest range, strong sympathetic vibration ("resonance") can be located in the chest; in lower middle voice, sensation gradually leaves the chest; in upper middle voice, the feeling is that "resonance" (sympathetic vibration) has moved upward; and in the upper range, sensation becomes more marked in areas of the head. These personal impressions have led to a number of tone-placement theories that confuse the *sensation* of the sounds of singing with the *source* of the sounds of singing. Knowledge of the causes of sympathetic vibration assists the teacher and singer to determine how the chiaroscuro tone is best achieved.

The three functioning parts of the vocal instrument are

1. the motor,
2. the vibrator, and
3. the resonator.

In response to airflow (motor) and vocal-fold approximation (vibrator), the laryngeally generated sound is modified by an acoustic filter (resonator): the vocal

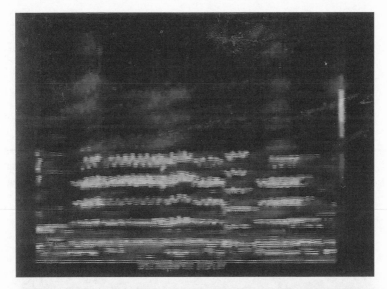

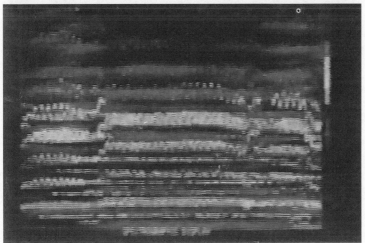

FIGURE 6.4. *Upper figure: spectrogram analysis (recorded performance) by soprano Renata Tebaldi singing a portion of the phrase "I giuramenti" from "Dove sono" (Le nozze di Figaro, Mozart). The first formant is shown at the bottom of the graph; the middle of the graph indicates the second formant, representing vowel definition; the third formant occupies the upper regions of the graph, with acoustic strength registered between 3000 and 4000 Hz. Wavy lines of the harmonic partials indicate vibrato.*

Lower figure: spectrogram analysis (recorded performance) of soprano Mirella Freni singing the phrase "profumo d'un fior" from the aria "Mi chiamano Mimì" (La bohème, Puccini). The first formant is shown at the bottom of the graph; the middle of the graph indicates the second formant, representing vowel definition; the third formant occupies the upper regions of the graph, with acoustic strength registered between 3000 and 4000 Hz. Wavy lines of the harmonic partials indicate vibrato. (Otto B. Schoepfle Vocal Arts Center, Oberlin Conservatory of Music, 1998)

FIGURE 6.5. *Upper figure: spectrogram analysis of Ethel Merman (recorded performance) singing "Bye, bye, baby, stop your yawnin'." The lower horizontal axis of the graph represents time; the left-hand axis represents frequency in Hz. Acoustic strength extends from the fundamental to more than 10,000 Hz. Straight lines of the harmonic partials indicate straight tone; wavy lines indicate vibrato.*

Lower figure: spectrogram analysis of Ethel Merman (recorded performance) singing "Don't cry baby, day will be dawnin'." The horizontal axis of the graph represents time; the left-hand axis represents frequency in Hz. Acoustic energy is registered from the fundamental to more than 10,000 Hz. Straight lines of the harmonic partials indicate straight tone; wavy lines indicate vibrato. (Otto B. Schoepfle Vocal Arts Center, Oberlin Conservatory of Music, 1998)

tract—the supraglottic system—that extends from the internal vocal folds to the external lips. The size and shape of the vocal tract determine its filtering properties. This resonator tract, consisting chiefly of the buccopharyngeal conduit (pharynx and mouth), is stimulated by the laryngeal source and determines the quality of the produced sound:[1] (1) [M]ovements of the articulators affect tube or cavity dimension in the vocal tract; (2) these shapes affect the resonances (that is, the filter function) of the vocal tract; and (3) this change in the filter affects what we hear. Contributors to vocal timbre include

1. the larynx, in its resonance capabilities and through its positions at different levels within the neck structure that affect responses of the resonator tube: (1) an elevated larynx shortens the distance between the vocal folds and the velar region; it shortens the distance of the resonator tube from the larynx to the lips, actions that thin out the timbre;(2) a depressed larynx lengthens the distance from the vocal folds to both the velum and the external lips and thickens timbre;(3) a relatively low stabilized larynx, varying greatly with the size of the larynx and the length of the neck, is the natural result of deep inhalation; it establishes and maintains normal spatial relationships among the vocal folds, the velum, and the lips, producing a consistency of timbre that sounds neither heavy nor lean;
2. the configuration of the pharyngeal wall: in complete inspiration, the pharyngeal wall undergoes slight expansion;
3. the position of the faucial arch and the velum: the faucial region and the velum tend to arch slightly during inspiration;
4. the shifting positions of the tongue: the body of the tongue shifts in response to vowel definition, and for the production of some consonants;
5. the action of the mandible (the jaw): the mandible assumes varying positions in vowel definition and in the rising scale;
6. the contour of the lips: the lips flexibly participate in articulatory movements; and
7. the configuration of the facial musculature as it relates to the zygomatic (cheek) region: the zygomatic region, together with the position of the lips and the mouth, affects shaping of the buccopharyngeal resonator.

Figure 6.6 indicates some points of articulation within the resonator system. The chief resonance chamber, comprising the mouth and the pharynx (buccopharyngeal cavity), is adjustable. The mouth and pharynx effectively make up a single room whose dimensions can be altered. For example, in the front vowels [i, ɪ, e, ɛ, ae, a], the pharynx gains prominence as a resonating space; by contrast, in the back vowels [ɑ, ɔ, o, ʊ, u], the mouth takes on added importance as a resonator. (In some phonetic systems [ɑ] is considered a neutral vowel, while in others it is thought to be the first of the back-vowel series.) The neutral vowels (ʌ and ə) are closer to the acoustic at-rest posture. (See fig. 6.7.)

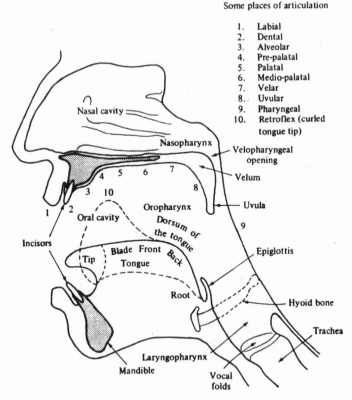

Some places of articulation

1. Labial
2. Dental
3. Alveolar
4. Pre-palatal
5. Palatal
6. Medio-palatal
7. Velar
8. Uvular
9. Pharyngeal
10. Retroflex (curled tongue tip)

FIGURE 6.6. *A schematic view indicating some places of articulation. (From Fred D. Minifie, Thomas J. Hixon, and Frederick Williams, eds.,* Normal Aspects of Speech, Hearing, and Language *[Englewood Cliffs, N.J.: Prentice-Hall, 1973], Allyn and Bacon. By permission.)*

Elevation of the front portion of the tongue distinguishes the lateral vowels; by contrast, in rounded vowels the anterior portion of the tongue is low and the posterior part elevated. The tongue moves flexibly for the formation of most consonants. Speech recognizability depends on the changing shapes of this resonator tube and on the articulatory action of the tongue and the lips. These shifting relationships form the essence of phonetic articulation in language communication. They control diction and timbre in singing. (See fig. 6.8.)

A significant role as an actual resonator is played by the larynx itself, and by areas directly adjacent to it.[2] (See fig. 6.9.) The ventricular sinuses (also called the laryngeal sinuses, or the sinuses of Morgagni) that lodge between the false and true vocal folds, and the piriform sinuses (pear-shaped spaces that lie between the wing of the thyroid cartilage and the laryngeal collar) may be of considerable importance in determining the chiaroscuro resonance balance of the singing voice.

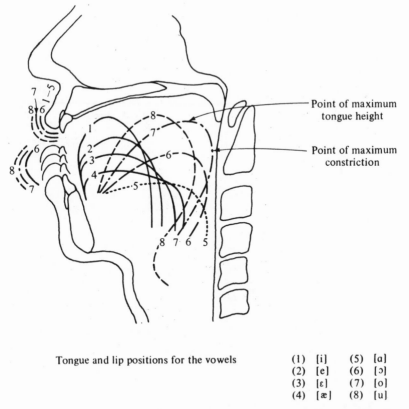

Point of maximum
tongue height

Point of maximum
constriction

Tongue and lip positions for the vowels

(1)	[i]	(5)	[ɑ]
(2)	[e]	(6)	[ɔ]
(3)	[ɛ]	(7)	[o]
(4)	[æ]	(8)	[u]

FIGURE 6.7. *A schematic view of tongue and lip positions for a number of vowels. (From Fred D. Minifie, Thomas J. Hixon, and Frederick Williams, eds.,* Normal Aspects of Speech, Hearing, and Language *[Englewood Cliffs, N.J.: Prentice-Hall, 1973], Allyn and Bacon. By permission.)*

The conviction of many singers and teachers of singing that the cavities of the head (sinuses) provide a major source of resonance is not supported by investigative evidence. It should be reiterated that the buccopharyngeal resonator track—the combined chambers of the mouth and pharynx—sometimes joined with the nasal cavities (only for nasal consonants and foreign-language nasal vowels), the larynx, and the piriform sinuses, comprise the resonance system of the voice. Although the chest itself cannot serve as a resonator, the subglottic area of the respiratory tract, including the trachea as far as the bronchial bifurcation (branching) at its base, may contribute to resonance in the low register of the voice. However, the precise contribution of the trachea, which has its own fixed resonance, remains unclear as regards the singing voice. Studies dealing with "tracheal pull" as a contributive element in sung phonation remain inconclusive.

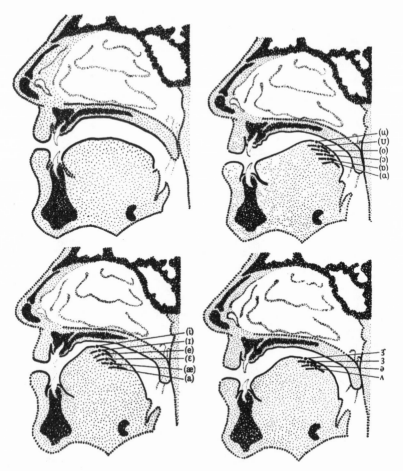

FIGURE 6.8. *Some spoken vowel postures (From C. Kantner and R. West,* Phonetics *[New York: Harper, 1960], Addison-Wesley Educational Publishers. By permission.)*

Because resonator-tract coupling serves as a filtering process of laryngeally produced tone, the manner in which the resonator tract is shaped largely determines the vowel, the timbre, and the sensations of resonance. Elaborate pedagogic systems have been devised for directing the tone into the sinuses, "up and over" into the forehead, into the masque, to the end of the nose, to the top of the head, into the back of the head, or down the spine. Tone, of course, cannot be placed. However, diverse sensations of sympathetic vibration do ensue from various configurations of resonator coupling and pitch location. One of the most extensive chapters in the history of comparative vocal pedagogy concerns divergent systems of "voice (or tone) placement." Some procedures devised for "tone placement" exist only in the realm of imagery. They have significance for their advocates, but they do not serve well for transfer of

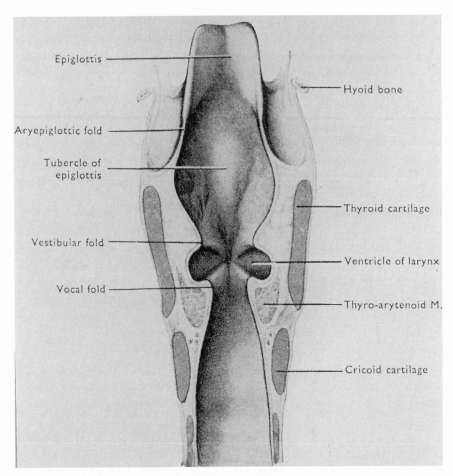

FIGURE 6.9. *Schematic sagittal view: hyoid bone, epiglottis, aryepiglottic fold, thyroid cartilage, vestibular fold (false vocal fold), ventricle of the larynx (sinus of Morgagni), true vocal fold, thyroarytenoid muscle, cricoid cartilage, and trachea.* (From G. J. Romanes, ed., Cunningham's Manual of Practical Anatomy, *vol. 2, 14th ed. [Oxford: Oxford University Press, 1977]. By permission.*)

information because these pedagogic systems try to make the body work in ways that are physiologically not possible. Attempts to "place" sound through localized controls inhibit efficient resonator coupling of the laryngeal, pharyngeal, buccal and nasal cavities.

Techniques for optimum vowel and resonance filtering that are in accordance with the rules of acoustic and physiologic function can be systematically devised and mastered. Voice acoustics and physiology are not in need of invention. It is not useful to supplant a major area of vocal technique (vowel tracking and resonance balancing) with hovering birds, floating pink clouds, rainbows, or balls bouncing on spraying fountains, nor with efforts to direct sound to nonexistent domes and imaginary holes in the head. Instruction expressed through inventive and imaginative language as to how the larynx and the buccopharyngeal resonator system are coordinated for singing is not only confusing but generally counterproductive. Factual information is much simpler.

There is no more logical way to develop a systematic pedagogy that produces desirable resonance balancing in the singing voice than to ground it on the acoustic properties of vowels and consonants. Communicative language is specific, and it is far less complex than privately devised theories of "tone placement." When the singer's imagination is free of arcane, nonfunctional physiologic and acoustic considerations, both technique and artistry move more quickly forward.

The two main causes of timbre distortion in singing are breath emission problems and an inability to coordinate the supraglottic resonator tract with the laryngeally generated vowel (failure to "track" the vowel with corresponding postures of lips, tongue, jaw, mouth, and pharynx). For all vowel sounds, the articulatory mechanism must be in synchronization with the laryngeal source. The physical formation of each vowel determines the distinctive shape that the vocal tract momentarily assumes during vowel differentiation procedures, thereby clarifying timbre.

Because of the prolonged duration of vowel definition in singing, accuracy in the tracking of the laryngeally produced vowel by the supraglottic resonator can be precise, and its production is learnable. Almost equally important is the proper phonetic formation for voiced and unvoiced consonants, a topic to be considered more fully in chapter 8.

A detailed presentation of the physical differences and similarities that produce families of phonemes exceeds the limits of this study. However, in learning to identify clear distinctions among language sounds, it is important for singers and teachers to know and to use the International Phonetic Alphabet (IPA). The IPA symbols for vowels, semi-vowels, and French vowel sounds, with model words in four languages essential to the singer, are shown in table 6.1.[3]

Consonants are of equal significance in arriving at balanced phonation during singing. They can be divided into those that have pitch (voiced) and those that do not (unvoiced). Pairs of consonants, one member voiced and the other unvoiced, are executed with similar tongue, lip, and jaw positions. During the training process, a singer needs to be aware of the physical locations of consonantal formations and to recognize how the execution of consonants may adversely influence the vowel that follows.

Classification of voiceless and voiced consonant pairs, nasal consonants, and several other unpaired voiced consonants, illustrated by IPA symbols, are indicated with corresponding model words in table 6.2.[4]

A simple run-through of the alphabet in most languages of the Western world identifies two tongue postures that are most involved in the production of vowels

Table 6.1. IPA Symbols for Vowels, Semi-vowels, and French Vowel Sounds

IPA Symbols	English	German	Italian	French
Vowels				
[i]	k<u>ee</u>n	L<u>ie</u>be	pr<u>i</u>ma	l<u>i</u>s
[ɪ]	th<u>i</u>n	<u>i</u>ch		
[e]	ch<u>a</u>os	L<u>e</u>ben	p<u>e</u>na	<u>é</u>t<u>é</u>, cri<u>e</u>r
[ɛ]	b<u>e</u>t	B<u>e</u>tt, G<u>ä</u>ste	t<u>e</u>mpo	<u>ê</u>tes, p<u>è</u>re n<u>ei</u>ge
[æ]	b<u>a</u>t			
[a]	t<u>a</u>sk (American)			p<u>a</u>rle
[ɑ]	f<u>a</u>ther	St<u>a</u>dt	c<u>a</u>mer<u>a</u>	r<u>a</u>s, <u>â</u>ge
[ɒ]	h<u>o</u>t (British)			
[ɔ]	s<u>o</u>ft, <u>a</u>ll	S<u>o</u>nne	m<u>o</u>rto	s<u>o</u>mme, j<u>o</u>li, v<u>o</u>tre
[o]	n<u>o</u>te	S<u>o</u>hn	n<u>o</u>n	b<u>eau</u>x, p<u>au</u>vre, gr<u>o</u>s
[ʊ]	n<u>oo</u>k	M<u>u</u>tter		
[u]	gn<u>u</u>, f<u>oo</u>l	M<u>u</u>t	<u>u</u>so	<u>ou</u>
[ʌ]	<u>u</u>p			
[ə]	(schwa) <u>a</u>head	g<u>e</u>tan		d<u>e</u>main
[y]	(approximates [i] plus [u]) m<u>ü</u>de			<u>u</u>ne
[ʏ]	(approximates [ɪ] plus [ʊ]) Gl<u>ü</u>ck			
[ø]	(approximates [e] plus [o]) sch<u>ö</u>n			p<u>eu</u>
[œ]	(approximates [ɛ] plus [ɔ]) K<u>ö</u>pfe			h<u>eu</u>re
Semi-vowels and glides				
[j]	<u>y</u>es	<u>j</u>a	pi<u>ù</u>, p<u>i</u>eno	l<u>i</u>on, p<u>i</u>ed
[w]	<u>w</u>ish		<u>u</u>omo, g<u>u</u>ida	m<u>oi</u>ns
[aɪ]	n<u>i</u>ce	[ae] M<u>ai</u>, <u>Ei</u>	[ai] m<u>ai</u>	
[aʊ]	h<u>ou</u>se	[ao] H<u>au</u>s	[au] <u>au</u>ra	
[eɪ]	w<u>ay</u>		[ei] dov<u>ei</u>	
[ɔɪ]	b<u>oy</u>	[ɔø] H<u>äu</u>ser, Kr<u>eu</u>z	[ɔi] vu<u>oi</u>	
[oʊ]	s<u>o</u>			
Vowel sounds peculiar to the French language				
[ã]				t<u>em</u>ps
[ɛ̃]				f<u>aim</u>, v<u>in</u>
[õ]				n<u>om</u>, l<u>ong</u>
[œ̃]				parf<u>um</u>, j<u>eun</u>

and of voiced and unvoiced consonant pairs. In languages chiefly encountered in the classical literature for singing (English, French, German, and Italian), unless there are orthodontic problems, the apex of the tongue remains in contact with the inner surface of the lower front teeth for the execution of all vowels. Similarly, the tongue stays in contact with the inner surface of the lower front teeth for the production of many consonants, such as [b], [p], [f], [v], [g], [k], [ʔ], [h], [m], [n], [ɲ], [ŋ], [s],

Table 6.2. IPA Symbols for Consonant Sounds

	Voiceless		Classification by Formation	Voiced	
Pairs[a]					
[p]–[b]	[p]	pope	bilabial	[b]	bob
[t]–[d]	[t]	tote	lingua-alveolar	[d]	dead
[k]–[g]	[k]	coke	velar	[g]	glug
[f]–[v]	[f]	fife	labiodental	[v]	valve
[θ]–[ð]	[θ]	think	linguadental	[ð]	the
[s]–[z]	[s]	cease	dental	[z]	zones
[ʃ]–[ʒ]	[ʃ]	Sh!	lingua-alveolar	[ʒ]	vision
[ç]–[b]	[ç]	ich (German)	palatal		
[x]–[ʁ]	[x]	ach (German)	velar	[ʁ]	Paris (French)
[h]–[ʔ]	[h]	ha-ha! (aspirate)	glottal	[ʔ]	uh-oh! (stroked glottal)
[tʃ]–[dʒ]	[tʃ]	chase	lingua-alveolar	[dʒ]	judgment
[ts]–[dz]	[ts]	tsetse	linguadental	[dz]	adds
Nasal consonants					
[m]			bilabial nasal		ma
[n]			alveolar nasal		no
[ŋ]			velar nasal		song
[ɲ]			palatal nasal		ogni (Italian), onion (English), agneau (French)
[ɱ]			nasal labio-dental		conforto (Italian)
Other voiced consonants					
[ʎ]					foglia (Italian)
[l]					lull
[ɹ]					rare (retroflex r, sometimes referred to as midwestern r)
[r]					very (single tap r, as in British speech)
[ř][c]					carro (Italian); Grund (German) (alveolar trill)

[a]Pairs of consonants, one un-voiced and the other voiced, are executed with similar tongue and lip positions.

[b][ç] is generally believed to be without a voiced counterpart.

[c] The symbol [ř] is used here, and in many phonetic sources, to represent the alveolar rolled r, because the IPA symbol for the trilled r [r] is used indiscriminately in many sources.

and [z]. For the majority of language sounds, this linguadental formation is the articulatory home base for the tongue. (Further consideration of the acoustic role played by consonants in adjusting the resonator tract will be undertaken when techniques for resonator balancing are discussed.) A linguadental position is normally the acoustic at-rest location of the tongue during silence and in the production of the neutral vowels uttered when one thinks aloud, as in "uh." In another frequent phonetic position that produces recognizable speech, the apex of the tongue finds itself in contact with the alveolar ridge (located behind the upper front teeth). For example, the consonants [d], [t], [dz], [l], [n] are alveolar in English, as are the single-flipped and the rolled [r].

Clean enunciation in speech and good diction in singing require articulatory exactitude. The vocal tract is not constructed to maintain a single shape through which all vowels and consonants are formed. In nonpathological speech, the resonator tract (the buccopharyngeal cavity) remains flexible during the production of communicative language. It would be illogical to retain the jaw and mouth near some one basic posture while speaking in any language, yet certain techniques of singing support that assumption. Most prominent among them are

1. maintaining a low jaw position,
2. trumpeting the lips (holding the lips and the jaw in the [ɔ] [aw] position),
3. squaring the lips and the jaw,
4. pulling downward on the platysma muscle,
5. retaining the smile position,
6. maintaining an elevation of the upper lip,
7. covering the upper teeth with the upper lip (pulling downward on the upper lip), and
8. covering the lower teeth with the lower lip.

These pedagogic tenets advocate minimal differentiations among vowel formations; they disregard normal phonetic responses to the shifting acoustic demands of ascending and descending pitch and of diverse dynamic levels. The singing voice is regarded as a fixed resonator although, by its physical nature, the voicing instrument is a flexible, nonfixated system. By retaining a single articulatory posture, diction accuracy is impeded. There is no fixed resonance in the vocal instrument such as exists in most other musical instruments; the resonation system of the vocal instrument does not parallel those of the horn, the trumpet, or the trombone, even though adjustments of players' buccopharyngeal cavities can complement the resonance of mechanical instruments. A cardinal rule for the singing voice is that there is no one ideal position of the mouth or jaw. It is the vowel, the consonant, the tessitura, and the intensity level that determine the degree of mouth aperture (mandibular movement).

Many lingering problems among preprofessional singers come from prior requests by choral conductors for the suppression of solo-voice timbre, so that no singer will "stick out" in the ensemble. A frequent quick fix for masking the individuality of voices in a choir is to have all the singers in the ensemble adopt the "idiot jaw" (hung jaw) posture. Singers are told to drop the jaw to achieve "space in the throat" and to "let the sound out." Choristers at times are also advised to mix breath in the tone as a means of curtailing resonance values ("start every sound with an initial feeling of airflow"). These methods remove upper harmonic partials from the spectrum, reducing all voices to one dimension of nonvibrant timbre. Although the dilemma of the preprofessional solo singer in the vocal ensemble remains a topic of major concern in academic settings, it can be dealt with here only in passing.

Choral sound is patently vocal sound; the same principles of efficient production apply to both the solo singer and the chorister. It should not be the aim of the choral conductor to *blend* vocal timbres by reducing all voices to one bland amateur color, but to *balance* them.[5] Fortunately, the belief that each voice must mimic a uniformly de-timbred quality in order to blend with other voices is losing ground within professional North American choral circles.

The principle of vocal-tract mobility was well recognized in the historic Italian school: *si canta come si parla* ("one sings as one speaks") and *chi pronuncia bene, canta bene* ("who enunciates well, sings well"). How these related principles are applied and modified in actual practice during singing will be a major part of the technical considerations that follow.

In classical singing it is essential that the vowel not undergo major phonetic change during its course of execution. Native English speakers tend to introduce diphthongization when singing in either their own or other languages. A major detriment to timbre on the part of many English-speaking singers (particularly North Americans) is the inclination to mirror running speech, thereby altering the acoustic nature of a sustained sung vowel. This problem must be addressed in the early years of voice study or it will forever plague the performer. Much of the time, money, and energy expended in professional coaching sessions for established singers consists of the elimination of language transition sounds (on-glides and off-glides) that are carried over from the rapid occurrences of speech into the more sustained sounds of singing. Regional speech habits and the lack of phonetic precision in spoken language do not support the *si canta come si parla* dictum unless one is speaking pure Tuscan, with its clean vowel definition and its lack of transition sounds. Therefore, during singing in all the languages (except in pop vocal idioms), the slurrings of colloquial speech should be eliminated. The duration factor in singing makes phonetic precision in all languages possible, achieving the phonetician's idealized exactitude of vowel and consonant formations.

As the singing scale ascends, levels of airflow and subglottic pressure do not precisely parallel those of the speaking range. Phonetic alteration required by *aggiustamento* (modification) of the vowel for mounting pitch in singing is unlike the events appropriate to the speaking range. Yet the principle of vocal-tract flexibility (vowel tracking) that produces language recognition undergirds supraglottic activity throughout all ranges of the singing voice.

EXAMPLE 6.1.

As previously mentioned, each vowel has its own distinctive laryngeal configuration that requires a corresponding vocal-tract configuration for the proper tracking
of that vowel. Regardless of changing pitch, the distribution of acoustic energy must
permit both accuracy of vowel differentiation and the *chiaroscuro* tone of the historic international school.

The concept in modern pedagogy of vowel tracking corresponds directly to the
historic ideal of vowel purity in the singing voice. Each successful acoustic event that
distinguishes the professional singing voice is the result of coordinated synergistic
action between the motor, the vibrator, and the supraglottic filter. The old Italian
rubric *si canta come si parla* finds verification in international contemporary spectrographic analyses of the resonant singing voice. Particularly in medium range, it is
possible to sing as one speaks. (Vowel modification as a device for scale unification
in ascending pitch will be considered when registration is discussed in chapter 10.)

One of the best ways to illustrate what remains stable about mouth and jaw postures during the production of a vowel series and what alters is to speak a simple
lateral-to-rounded (front to back) vowel sequence such as [i–e–ɑ–e–i] while observing facial postures in a hand mirror, then immediately to sing the pattern in speech
range (still looking in the mirror) using the same shifting buccal positions. Then one
speaks and sings the reverse vowel sequence [ɑ–e–i–e–ɑ], continuing the mirror
check. These sequences ought to be sung in several keys in the speech-inflection
range with nearly the identical vowel definition that occurs in speech (avoiding diphthongization, of course). Normal flexibility of mouth, lips and jaw—neither buccal
nor mandibular fixation—is the aim. If the mouth is held in the lateral position of
[i] as the vowel series [i–e–ɑ–e–i] progresses, the other vowels, particularly [ɑ], will
be distorted. Conversely, if the open-mouth position for [ɑ] is kept for the production of the vowels [i] and [e] during the order [ɑ–e–i–e–ɑ], distortion will take place
in the *lateral* vowels. In both cases, pitch will tend to lose exactitude (ex. 6.1).

A lateral and a rounded vowel should be alternated in a pattern of moderately
changing pitch levels such as a simple broken-triad pattern. Example 6.2 begins with
the vowel progression [e–ɑ] in sequence through the keys of F, G♭, and G and then
reverses the vowel order to an [ɑ–e] series.

Vowel sequences should alternate over a broken arpeggio figure (ex. 6.3) in several near keys such as E♭, E, F, G♭, and G, thereafter descending to the key of D. Combinations of lateral and front vowels ought to be used: [ɛ–ɔ]; [ɛ–o]; [e–u]; [ɑ–o];

EXAMPLE 6.2.

EXAMPLE 6.3.

[ɑ–ɔ]; [ɑ–u]; [i–ɑ]; [i–o]; [i–o; and [i–u]. It is essential, when vowel and pitch patterns change, to keep resonance constant without loss of vowel definition. Hand-mirror monitoring of phonetic postures develops awareness of the changing positions (never to be exaggerated) of lips, mouth, and jaw necessary for accurate vowel definition. A good maxim with regard to vowel definition is "move only what needs to be moved."

Vowel definition occurs within small articulatory confines. The age-old adage of the international Italian school, *raccogliere la bocca* ("collect the mouth"), sums up the principle of vowel tracking for singing. The singer must give up all inefficient learned techniques of buccopharyngeal fixation. When in the speech-inflection range, she must define the vowels within *una bocca raccolta* ("a collected mouth"). In *aggiustamento* (vowel modification adjustment for pitches above speech level) the mouth will open, but the integrity of vowel posture will still be maintained.

Throughout these vowel-definition exercises, the aim is to combine vowel integrity with the well-balanced resonance of the *chiaroscuro* timbre. In order to do so, the articulatory parts of the speaking and singing mechanism must be allowed to alter flexibly.

Example 6.4 should begin in the key of E♭, progress chromatically through the tonalities of E, F, G♭, G, A♭, A, B♭, and B, and then move downward by semitone to the original key. The two indicated vowel patterns [ɑ–o–i–o–e] and [i–o–ɑ–o–e] may be sung throughout the entire key sequence either separately or alternately. Then other combinations of lateral and rounded vowels such as [ɔ–ɛ–i–ɔ–ɛ], [ɛ–ɔ–o–ɔ–ɛ] and [i–ʊ–ɔ–ʊ–i] are introduced.

It is beneficial to extend this vowel-changing series over an arpeggiated figure, with rhythmic accentuation now placed on the fifth of the scale, not on the upper-octave note. By accenting the fifth rather than the octave (retaining the same vowel for the 5–8–5 portion of the arpeggio), the inclination to strike the top of the arpeggio

EXAMPLE 6.4.

a. [ɑ - o - i - o - e]   [ɑ - o - i - o - e]   [ɑ - o - i - o - e]   [ɑ - o - i - o - e]
b. [i - o - ɑ - o - e]   [i - o - ɑ - o - e]   [i - o - ɑ - o - e]   [i - o - ɑ - o - e]

EXAMPLE 6.5.

a. [ɑ - o, i,_____ o - e]   [ɑ - o, i,_____ o - e]   [ɑ - o, e,_____ o - e]
b. [i - o, ɑ,_____ o - e]   [i - o, ɑ,_____ o - e]   [i - o, ɑ,_____ o - e]

EXAMPLE 6.6.

Some - how I feel that Thou__ art near, Though there is naught a -

round; Some - how I hear Thy soft__ sweet voice, Though there is not a sound,

aggressively is avoided. Tonalities should proceed upward from E♭ through G, then descend to D.

The aria and song literatures themselves provide innumerable sources for concentrating on the avoidance of vowel distortion and diphthongization. An excellent exercise for the English-speaking soprano who may need to concentrate on the elimination of habitual diphthongization can be found in the simple melodic setting of a text filled with diphthongs (ex. 6.6). "*A Memory*," by Rudolf Ganz, is useful as a teaching device because the text is initially intoned on one pitch, thereby avoiding the complexity of frequent intervallic shiftings and directing attention solely to phonetic sequencing of the syllables. The initial vowel of each diphthongized syllable should be elongated ("some*how*, *I* feel that *thou* art *near*, *though there* is naught *around*"), with the glides of the vowels coming only at the moment of termination of the syllable.

Teachers of singing rightly consider phrases in Italian ideally suited for alerting the singer's ear to vowel exactitude. For young singers, no better exercise in retaining pure vowel definition in the alternation of back and front vowels can be devised

EXAMPLE 6.7.

than the opening phrases of an *aria antica* universally known to singers, "*Caro mio ben*" (usually attributed to Tommaso Giordani, but most probably composed by Giuseppe Giordani): "Caro mio ben, credimi almen, senza di te languisce il cor" should be executed in several keys. It may be advisable first to sing the designated phrases using only the inherent vowels, then to return to the text as written, with its quickly occurring consonants. The calm movement of the bel canto phrases encourages conscious attention to exactitude in vowel definition and resonance balancing. (Incidentally, the singer must be careful not to use a roll on the [r] of *caro*, or she will be singing "wagon.")

For all categories of soprano (not only those who might sing the entire role) who have already established good *appoggio*, phrases excerpted from "*Ah! non credea mirarti*" from Amina's famous aria (*La sonnambula*, Bellini) serve admirably as a study in back-front vowel definition (as well as in bel canto line). The text "Ah! non credea mirarti si presto estinto, o fiore, passati al par d'amore, che un giorno solo, . . . ah! sol durò" may be transposed through a series of neighboring keys to lower and higher pitch levels (see ex. 6.7).

Equally beneficial as a study in the juxtaposition of lateral and rounded vowels are the magnificent Bellini phrases beginning with "Raggio del tuo sembiante, Ah! parmi il brillar del giorno: ah! l'aura che spira intorno mi sembra un tuo sospir," in Giulietta's aria from *I Capuleti e i Montecchi* (see ex. 6.8).

It would not be possible to devise a more grateful study for the disciplining of soprano vowel definition than occurs with the rounded and lateral vowel relationships in a passage from Lucia's familiar first-act duet with Alisa (*Lucia di Lammermoor*, Donizetti), beginning at "Quando rapito in estasi del più cocente ardore" (see ex. 6.9).

Before we leave the topic of supraglottic action during singing, a word regarding the application of contemporary voice science to voice pedagogy is in order. Current

EXAMPLE 6.8.

Rag - gio__del tuo sem - bian - te, ah! par - mi il bril-lar_____ del__

gior - no: ah! i'au - ra che spi - ra in - tor - no mi sembra un tuo so-

spir, ah! l'au - ra che spi - ra in - tor - no mi__ sem - bra

EXAMPLE 6.9.

Quan - do ra - pi - to in e - sta - si del più co-cen - te ar - do - re,

col fa - vel - lar del co - re__ mi giu - ra e - ter - na fè, e - ter - na fè,

spectrographic and fiberoptic studies verify basic tenets of the historic international school of vocalism.

Some recently devised techniques based on interpretations of the findings from the fields of voice science and vocal therapy have not proved useful in training the singing voice. An example can be found in the singer suffering from tongue and throat tensions who is told to insert a fist into her mouth as a way to reduce laryngeal tension, or to insert three fingers vertically to obtain the best phonatory position. Another is that of the voice therapist who tells the singer to yawn in order to "open the throat," and to forcefully use the diaphragm as a piston to produce "flow phonation." No matter what their value in speech therapy, the injurious ramifications of these counsels when applied to the tasks of singing must not be overlooked. The assumption is made that if the pharyngeal wall is consciously spread and the larynx lowered, laryngeal tension will be reduced. Disregarded is the fact that the yawn is not intended as a sustained maneuver for the kind of phonation that occurs during singing. Retaining the posture of the yawn during speech or song induces hyperfunction in the submandibular musculature and precludes natural-sounding voice quality. Purposeful attempts to make space locally in the buccopharyngeal resonator tube induce phonatory tensions in the palatopharyngeus and palatoglossus muscles, in the faucial arch, and in the digastric, mylohyoid, geniohyoid, and genioglossus muscles. Efforts to increase the level of airflow, although useful as a corrective procedure in certain forms of pressed spoken phonation, are notoriously detrimental to the timbre of the classical singing voice.

In singing one must coordinate the acoustic and physiologic events of vowel definition while at the same time taking into account the relationships (and adaptations) of speaking to the singing voice. The essential modifications of these occurrences form the substance of voice pedagogy. Only when these factors are coordinated can balanced resonance, with the harmonic partials that give the professional voice its characteristic chiaroscuro timbre, be fully realized.

A logical step for the soprano who has stabilized *appoggio* breath management, who can move the voice with ease, and who has established a secure resonance balance through clearly defined vowels is to turn to groups of pilot consonants that assist in maintaining dynamic resonance balance throughout the changing acoustic maneuvers present in every sung text.

7

Nasal Continuants as Assists
in Resonance Balancing

Although the words *vowelization* and *vocalization* share a common semantic origin that testifies to the centrality of the vowel in the production of vocal sound, it is the consonant that brings language intelligibility to both speech and song. No matter how accurate vowel tracking is during singing, good diction is impossible without clean, precise consonants.

Consonants may be classified in several ways, chiefly in accordance with physical formation. Most consonants fall into one of several categories:

1. bilabial (lips closed),
2. linguadental (tongue in contact with the teeth),
3. labiodental (upper teeth in contact with lower lip),
4. alveolar (tongue touching the ridge behind the upper front teeth),
5. velar (the sudden release of breath between tongue and velum), and
6. nasal (lowered velum—open velopharyngeal port).

Most consonants are teamed as pairs, one voiced, the other unvoiced. (Grouping of consonants by pairs has already been encountered; see table 6.2.) For example, the bilabial [b] is generated with the vocal folds adducted (closed) whereas the bilabial [p], although formed at the same phonetic location as [b], is produced with abducted (parted) vocal folds. Both are plosives. The sibilant [s], with its hissing sound, is unvoiced, while its sister [z] is voiced.

Before turning to the practical application of nonnasal consonants as assists in adjusting the vocal tract, a look must be taken at the role of nasal consonants. With regard to velar action, each nasal [m, n, ɲ, ŋ] that figures in the singing voice has its own mechanical variation. Of the four, [m] provides the most mouth resonance.

It should be kept in mind that velopharyngeal closure, in which the velum touches the pharyngeal wall, closing off the port into the nasal cavity, is the rule for the production of all vowels in the major western European languages, except for the French and Portuguese nasal vowels. The supraglottic resonator system is conjoined with the nasal cavity (through velar lowering) only to allow the introduction of nasality.

The upper illustration of figure 7.1, (a), indicates the posture of the soft palate in relationship to Passavant's ridge during quiet breathing. (For better viewing, the nasopharyngeal wall has been artificially pulled backward.) The X-ray photo in (b) indicates a lowered velum, as occurs in one form of nasality. The photo in (c) displays a degree of velopharyngeal closure in nonnasal phonation.

Of particular importance to the singer is the location and extent of any spatial arrangement in the velar region during the indicated gesture of velopharyngeal closure. Clearly, it is not possible to create a resonating dome at the back of the throat wall; elevation of the velum is limited by the structure of the fixed surrounding regions. An upward dimpling maneuver of the soft palate is apparent just in advance of the uvula (fig. 7.1), revealing that a limited increase of pharyngeal space—but anterior to the pharyngeal wall—can occur.

Studies on nasality as it occurs during nasal consonants disclose variable degrees of velar lowering and of velopharyngeal closure. During the singing of a series of nasal consonants, the soft palate, in its relationship to the nasopharyngeal wall, tends to be in a lower position with [m], [n], and [ɲ] than it is with [ŋ]. That is, generally in singing, the nasal consonants [m], [n], and [ɲ] indicate less velopharyngeal closure than does the consonant [ŋ].

During the singing of a series of nasal consonants, the buccal resonator (the mouth), the pharyngeal resonator (comprising the laryngopharynx, the oropharynx, and the nasopharynx), and the nose (the nasal cavities encompassing the nasal fossae and the nostrils) are conjoined. The nasal continuant [n] is produced by retaining most of the resonation space of the mouth, but with the front portion excluded as a resonator by the elevation of the tongue as it contacts the alveolar ridge and by employing the pharynx and the nasal cavities. Sound, of course, emerges through the nose.

In the third nasal continuant [ɲ] (as in English *onion*, French *oignon*, and Italian *ogni*), the elevated mid-region of the tongue body is in contact with the hard palate. As a result, the forward portion of the mouth is eliminated as a resonator, while the pharynx and the nasal cavities continue to be coupled to the rest of the mouth. Because the front portion of the mouth is blocked off by tongue elevation, sound must emerge by way of the nose.

With the fourth nasal [ŋ], the velum and the tongue close off the mouth entirely. Only the pharynx and the nasal cavities contribute to supraglottic resonance. As mentioned above, the nose provides the sole exit route for the sound.

Because each of these four nasals is a voiced consonant capable of prolongation, they are grouped together as nasal continuants. For production of the nasals, as is the case with all voiced consonants, the vocal folds are adducted. In both speaking and singing, the varying shape of the resonator tract associated with each of the four nasals produces a distinctive proprioceptive sensation for each singer; every nasal

A

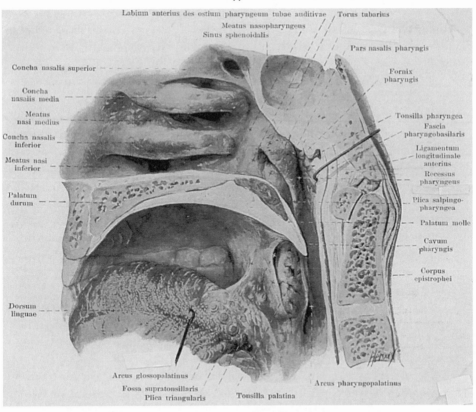

Labium anterius des ostium pharyngeum tubae auditivae · Torus tubarius

Meatus nasopharyngeus
Sinus sphenoidalis

Pars nasalis pharyngis

Concha nasalis superior

Fornix
pharyngis

Concha
nasalis media

Meatus
nasi medius

Tonsilla pharyngea

Fascia
pharyngobasilaris

Concha nasalis
inferior

Ligamentum
longitudinale
anterius

Meatus nasi
inferior

Recessus
pharyngeus

Palatum
durum

Plica salpingo-
pharyngea

Palatum molle

Cavum
pharyngis

Corpus
epistrophei

Dorsum
linguae

Arcus glossopalatinus

Arcus pharyngopalatinus

Fossa supratonsillaris
Plica triangularis

Tonsilla palatina

B

C

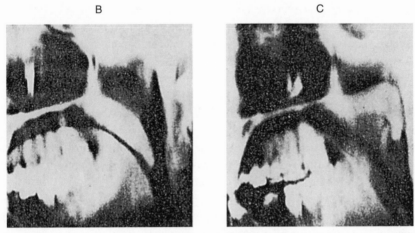

FIGURE 7.1. *(a) View of the palate and the velopharyngeal region (redrawn from Walter Spalteholz, Leipzig:* Handatlas der Anatomie des Menschen, *1933); (b) open velopharyngeal port in a nasal phonation; (c) closure gesture of velopharyngeal port in a non-nasal phonation (redrawn from* Research Potentials in Vocal Physiology, *ed. Brewer [Syracuse, N.Y.: State University of New York Press, 1964]).*

continuant "feels" as if it is in a somewhat different location. These shifting sensations in the head result from sympathetic vibration chiefly conducted by the bony skull.

For most singers, [m] induces vibratory sensations around the lips and at the base of the nose. The sympathetic vibrations of the consonant [n] are often more centrally located in the zygomatic (cheek) region and at the anterior portion of the hard palate. Its near neighbor, [ɲ], produces sensations that seem to be situated along the hard palate and in the upper portion of the face and head, whereas for most singers [ŋ] feels more completely centered in the head, with sensations extending into upper regions of the skull.

Nasal continuants are widely used as resonance balancing agents in all classical vocal pedagogies of western Europe and North America because they elicit strong sensations. It is largely the responses effected by the production of nasals that have contributed to theories of "tone placement." Although pedagogically often based on misinformation as to the acoustic properties of sound, location sensations have practical pedagogic worth.

Over a span of decades, it has been noted by researchers and writers that nasal consonants instigate specific spectral results.[2] These sensations assist the singer in achieving desirable relationships between the fundamental pitch and its harmonic partials.

Hypotheses regarding the influence of nasals on resonance balancing can be verified through spectral analysis (spectrography). For example, in the speaking voice the consonant [m] induces strong acoustic responses in several parts of the spectrum: around 250 Hz, 1000 Hz, 3000 Hz, and 4000 Hz. The same phenomena hold true for the singing voice. Other nasals show similar areas of acoustic strength. (Soubrettes will exhibit these phenomena at slightly higher pitches than do dramatics.)

The consonant [m] is of special value to the singer in uniting resonance balancing to breath management (the *appoggio*). As was mentioned earlier, for formation of the bilabial [m] the lips are closed. The rate of breath emission is reduced, because humming [m] requires air to exit through the nasal cavity rather than by the more direct mouth route. During the singing of the sustained phoneme [m], the singer becomes aware of the relationship between the stability of the anterior-lateral-dorsal abdominal wall and the reduction of airflow. At the same time, coupling of buccopharyngeal and nasal cavity resonators is spontaneously accomplished.

With soprano voices of all sizes [m] serves both as an efficient coupler of resonator tract contributors and as a device for increasing perception of the *appoggio* breath management required for the sustained sounds of singing (see chapter 4).

Exercises dealing with nasal continuants should first be executed on patterns in the lower middle range. The singer becomes aware of the amount of contact among the muscles of the *appoggio* maneuver when producing a vibrant sound. Even in lower middle register, energization for singing goes much beyond the demands of spoken phonation.

EXAMPLE 7.1.

EXAMPLE 7.2.

Example 7.1 offers a typical use of the nasal continuant [m] for uniting good breath management, freedom of laryngeal function, and resonator coupling. The singer turns from humming to voweling on the same pattern and at the same dynamic level, while retaining the *appoggio* awareness.

Subsequently, a pattern alternating the continuant [m] with a vowel should be introduced (ex. 7.2). The purpose of this exercise is to allow resonance balancing (the chiaroscuro equilibrium among formants) to remain as operative during the singing of the subsequent vowel as on the nasal phoneme.

To ensure that nasality does not intrude during singing of the vowel, the singer should hold the nostrils closed from time to time (only on the vowel, not for the nasal, of course). This is a centuries-old technique. If undesirable air passes through the nose on the vowel while the nostrils are held closed—which means some nasality is continuing—it will become markedly apparent to a discriminating ear. Closing off the nostrils ensures that the velum is sufficiently raised to complete velopharyngeal closure for the vowel and that a full resonance balance is present.

It is not advisable for the singer to attempt to locally pull upward on the velum, because when the nasal port is closed for vowel production, the velum already is elevated (see fig. 7.1c). Faucial and velar elevations occur automatically in reaction to increased intensity and ascending pitch levels.

The same pattern should be executed with the nasal continuant [n] and a vowel (ex. 7.3). This is followed with the nasal continuant [ɲ] and a subsequent vowel (ex. 7.4). Finally, the pattern is sung with the nasal continuant [ŋ] and a succeeding vowel (ex. 7.5).

For the next systematic step in developing discernment of clean differentiation among nasals and nonnasals, the nasal continuant should be united to the vowel in

EXAMPLE 7.3.

[n - a,   n - a,   n - a,   n - a,   n - a]

EXAMPLE 7.4.

[ɲ - a,   ŋ - a,   ŋ - a,   ŋ - a,   - a]

EXAMPLE 7.5.

[ŋ - a,   ŋ - a,   ŋ - a,   ŋ - a,   - a]

a single syllabic phonation. The nasal now serves as a pilot resonance adjuster to the vowel that it introduces (ex. 7.6). Beginning in the tonality of D, the patterns should progress upward by semitone to the key of G♭, then descend to the key of D♭.

A disturbing tendency in the singing of all languages is the intrusion of nasal transition sounds as the singer approaches or leaves neighboring nasal phonemes. The singer herself, particularly the North American with a high rate of regional nasality in the speaking voice, may be unaware of the problem.

The selection of a few passages for assistance in the elimination of unwanted nasality in nonnasals can be productive. Purcell's "*Man, Man, Man, Is for the Woman Made*" is an example (ex. 7.7). As an exercise, the passage should be sung slowly; the soprano occludes the nostrils on the vowels between the two nasal consonants ([m] and [n]) in each syllable to be certain that nasality does not continue into the vowel. (Of course, as previously mentioned, there must be no occlusion of the nostrils during production of the nasal continuants.) Then the passage is sung up to performance tempo, making certain that nasals and nonnasals act independently.

From Despina's "Una donna a quindici anni dee saper ogni gran moda" (*Così fan tutte,* Mozart) comes another practical example of how repeated nasal consonants sometimes may get a soprano into trouble when she is singing the ensuing vowels. As with the Purcell excerpt of example 7.7, this passage should first be taken slowly, the singer checking against nasality in the vowels by occluding the nostrils on the vowels. Then she should perform the phrase at proper tempo, with nostrils unoccluded.

EXAMPLE 7.6.

EXAMPLE 7.7.

Man, man, man, is for the wo-man made, And the wo-man made for man.

In contrast to Despina's lighthearted 6/8, the slower setting of "*Alma mia*" (Handel), sung in traditional transposition for soprano voice, offers another example of the need to guard against transition sounds as the nasal consonants are approached and left. In "*Alma mia, sì, sol tu sei la mia gloria, il mio diletto,*" the singer must be on guard against the continuation of nasality on the second syllable of the word *alma* as it heads toward the first syllable of the word *mia*. She must also avoid transition sounds as she approaches the clustering of the consonants [l] and [m] on *alma* and *il mio diletto*.

The nasal continuant [ɲ] (as in the English words *union* and *onion*, the French *oignon*, and the Italian *ogni*) has already been briefly encountered in example 7.6. It is a pilot consonant (an initial phonatory gesture) that can be useful in adjusting the

EXAMPLE 7.8.

EXAMPLE 7.9.

resonator tract. A series of syllables in which both [ɲ] and [m] appear (*ogni uomo*) is illustrated in example 7.8. These patterns are transposable. Combining several nasals into repetitive patterns (e.g., ***ogni ignudo***) can also prompt resonance sensations associated with well-balanced vocal timbre, as in example 7.9.

In general, these exercises should begin in comfortable middle-voice range, then gradually be extended into both higher and lower tonalities.

Eventually a singer should be able to vocalize comfortably on all nasals throughout most of the scale. Proper breath management adjustments for the ascending scale can thereby be detected. However, because of the necessity to keep the mouth closed when humming, sopranos often are reluctant to use the [m] nasal in upper range, where the mouth appropriately wants to open more when singing the vowels. In such cases the [n] and the [ŋ] may be more genial. For example, in the Villa-Lobos "*Bachianas brasileiras no. 5,*" it may be wisest to substitute either [n] or [ŋ] for the indicated [m]. The writing itself is a good exercise in extending humming sounds into the upper range (ex. 7.10). A soprano should experiment with singing the passage on [m], [n], and [ŋ]. (The nasal [ɲ] is too difficult to execute in sustained phonation to be useful here.)

When singing French, it is important to permit nasal intrusion into vowel sound only on the nasal continuant and on the four French nasal vowels (see table 6.1). Both native French singers and non-French singers of the mélodie must be careful not to introduce nasality into the nonnasals. The age-old standard check against nasality suggested above—holding the nostrils closed on nonnasals—is especially of merit in ensuring the elimination of undesirable nasality in nonnasal syllables that follow French nasal vowels.

A common fault surfaces in the singing of French texts when a performer immediately introduces the same degree of nasality on nasalized syllables of long musical duration as would normally occur were those syllables to follow the fast rhythms of speech. Many singers, particularly North American and British, lower the velum

Example 7.10.

Example 7.11.

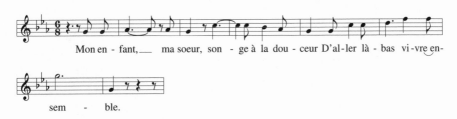

Mon en - fant,___ ma soeur, son - ge à la dou - ceur D'al-ler là - bas vi-vre en-

sem - ble.

at the commencement of all French nasal-vowel syllables, regardless of their metric duration. In current elegant classical singing of French, nasality is introduced only near the termination of a sustained nasal syllable, not at its inception; the concluding nasal sound then takes on the property of a delayed diphthong.

The opening phrases of Duparc's "*L'invitation au voyage*" offer a clear example of differences between the sustained singing of nasal French-language syllables and their occurrence in speech (ex. 7.11). The singer should be aware that, because of their briefer setting, the syllables *mon* and *en-* will be more quickly nasalized in this mélodie than will the syllables *-fant* and *songe*, which are given longer duration by the composer. The two nasal syllables of the word ***ensemble*** occur in Duparc's setting as an eighth note at F_5 and a dotted half note at G_5. The short note on the syllable *en-* first syllable of *ensemble*) ought to be immediately nasalized, whereas the sustained syllable *-sem-* should not be nasalized until near its point of termination. The same holds true for the nasal syllable in the word *resemble.* It is aesthetically unpleasant and does not improve sung French diction to introduce sustained honking noises; doing so does not sound "more French." The nasometer, an instrument that records degrees of nasality in phonation, is remarkably useful in measuring differences in duration between spoken and sung French nasal vowels as well as in identifying undesirable nasal intrusion into all nonnasals during singing.

For some singers, humming does not induce freedom. Usually, an inability to hum, especially in the upper middle and upper ranges, is an indication that tensions related to basic vocal production remain unsolved. A return to breath management (onset, release, and breath renewal), agility, and vowel-definition exercises are then in order.

8

Nonnasal Consonants as Assists in Adjustment of the Resonator Tract

A SINGER WHO IS UNAWARE OF THE PHONETIC FORMATIONS OF NON-nasal consonants is denied a rich source of practical assistance. Just as nasal continuants can be useful as pilot consonants for adjusting the resonator tract, so can nonnasal consonants. Formation of nonnasal consonant pairs was discussed in chapter 6. This chapter considers how nonnasal consonants can bear on balancing resonance in the singing voice.

As we have seen, [b–p] is a bilabial consonant pair. Both of these consonants have phonetic aspects that assist singers in adjusting the vocal tract for favorable resonance. Because they are produced with closed mouth, these consonants provide corrective help for singers who erroneously attempt to "open" the throat at inhalation by hanging the jaw or by breathing through a particular vowel shape. Jaw-droppers quickly learn that it is not necessary to place the mouth in a predetermined non-phonatory position for proper inhalation. They see how foolish it looks, how un-natural it feels, and how unpleasant the resultant sound is when they hang the jaw as though regurgitating, an actual request in one bizarre pedagogy. (Regurgitation does not open the throat, it closes it, so that the bolus [food mass] can be expelled from the esophagus.)

A second reason for making use of the consonants [b] and [p] is that they inhibit airflow in advance of the onset of sound. Both of these consonants serve as an antidote to breathy phonation.

The third reason for using the bilabials [b] and [p], produced directly at the lip bastion, is to get rid of unnecessary adjustments in the velar region. With the voiced consonant [b], place the forefinger in light contact with the surface of the closed lips so that the singer becomes aware of sympathetic vibration at the lips. Use of [b] and [p] as pilot consonants can be helpful in correcting forced elevation of the velum.

Now and again the soprano ought to inhale through the nose, then sing single syllables on various vowel combinations prefaced by [b] or [p] (ex. 8.1). With sopranos

EXAMPLE 8.1.

    a. [be-ba, be-ba, be]   [ba-be, ba-be, ba]
    b. [pe-pa, pe-pa, pe]   [pa-pe, pa-pe, pa]
    c. [pe-ba, pe-ba, pe]   [ba-pe, ba-pe, ba]

EXAMPLE 8.2.

who tend to produce opaque and internalized timbre, these procedures can be useful in recovering chiaroscuro tone. Both psychologically and physiologically, through their frontal formation, the bilabials can correct the loss of upper partials that is characterized by hooty "tube-tone" vocal production. The pattern of example 8.1 should begin in lower middle voice, progress through upper middle voice, and subsequently descend to lower voice.

Poulenc, in "*Ba, be, bi, bo, bu*" (*La courte paille*), supplies a charming exercise that plays on the voiced bilabial [b] as well as on the occasional unvoiced bilabial [p] (ex. 8.2). It can happily be transposed to a series of neighboring tonalities. During its execution, the soprano becomes aware of what bilabial closure achieves vocally.

Many problems of resonance balancing happen because the singer

1. places the apex of the tongue at the roots of the teeth rather than in contact with the inner surface of the lower front teeth,
2. pulls the tongue back from contact with the teeth, in a retroflex position,
3. curls the apex of the tongue upward and backward into the mouth,
4. holds the body of the tongue lower on one side than the other (so that opposite sides of the tongue groove are at different angles),
5. bunches up the body of the tongue in the middle (producing abnormal space at each side of the tongue), or
6. retains the lateral portions of the tongue in contact with the upper molars in an exaggerated [i] position, regardless of the vowel.

EXAMPLE 8.3.

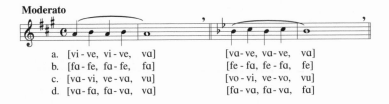

    a. [vi - ve, vi - ve,   va]   [va - ve, va - ve,   va]
    b. [fa - fe, fa - fe,   fa]   [fe - fa, fe - fa,   fe]
    c. [va - vi, ve - va,   vu]   [vo - vi, ve - vo,   vu]
    d. [va - fa, fa - va,   va]   [fa - va, fa - va,   fa]

EXAMPLE 8.4.

        Va   vi - a!___   Vi - va la ve-ra ver - i - tà!

The tongue is the chief vector in determining buccopharyngeal shaping. It is a bundle of muscles with potential for developing tensions during both rapid and sustained phonation; for that reason, tongue flexibility exercises are beneficial for all singers. Because tongue, hyoid bone, and larynx are an anatomical unit, tension in the tongue may affect laryngeal activity as well as linguistic articulation.

It will be remembered from the section on vowel formation and vowel differentiation (chapter 6) that during the progression from lateral through rounded vowels (front through back), the apex of the tongue lodges at the acoustic at-rest position regardless of changes in degrees of elevation or lowering by the tongue body for vowel definition.

During singing, pairs of labiodental consonants may be used to retain or reestablish normal phonetic postures. Of special merit is the [v–f] consonant pair. A pattern such as that in example 8.3 can be of value for two significant reasons:

1. attention is diverted away from the pharynx and the larynx, and
2. the tongue is placed in contact with the inner surface of the lower front teeth, where it belongs for all subsequent vowels and for a large number of consonants.

As in example 8.1, these patterns should be executed in ascending and descending tonalities while observing the postures of lips, mouth, and tongue in a hand mirror.

Occasional Italian-language patterns, such as *viva la vita!* sung on a single pitch, or expressions like *va via!* and *viva la vera verità!* (ex. 8.4), spoken at first in normal inflection range, can prepare for the tongue flexibility required to sing literature passages. These expressions should then be sung rapidly in a variety of tonalities.

EXAMPLE 8.5.

```
a. [vre - vra, vre - vra,   vre]        [vra - vre, vra - vre,   vra]
b. [fre - fra, fre - fra,   fre]        [fra - fre, fra - fre,   fra]
c. [vri - vre, vra - vro,   vru]        [fri - fre, fra, fro,    fru]
```

EXAMPLE 8.6.

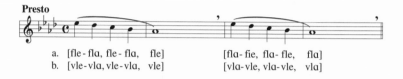

```
a. [fle - fla, fle - fla,   fle]        [fla - fie, fla - fle,   fla]
b. [vle - vla, vle - vla,   vle]        [vla - vle, vla - vle,   vla]
```

EXAMPLE 8.7.

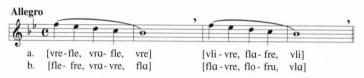

```
a. [vre - fle, vra - fle,   vre]        [vli - vre, fla - fre,   vli]
b. [fle - fre, vra - vre,   fla]        [fla - vre, flo - fru,   vla]
```

Both consonant and vowel formations keep the apex of the tongue in contact with the inner surface of the lower front teeth (not at the roots of the teeth, not elevated, and not pulled back). To be guarded against is the frequent tendency among English-language singers to pull the tongue lazily away from this phonetic home base when moving from the consonant to the vowel. Precise integrity of the two phonemes must prevail.

In executing the [v–f] consonant pair, most singers prefer the voiced [v] to the unvoiced [f]. However, through its high level of fricative airflow, unvoiced [f] can markedly increase a singer's awareness of the proper location for the tongue apex.

Once the tongue has been conditioned to remain in desirable contact with the inner surface of the lower front teeth, consonants formed at the alveolar ridge, such as the single-flipped [r] and [l], should be joined with the consonants [v] and [f]. (The singer must make certain that for [l] the tongue is in contact with the *upper* area of the upper front teeth, not positioned at the hard palate.

North American singers generally have sluggish tongue action, carried over from casual regional speech. Following a sung alveolar consonant, they may experience difficulty in returning quickly to the acoustic at-rest tongue-apex posture. Rapid patterns for inducing tongue freedom, such as those of examples 8.5, 8.6, and 8.7, should be a brief part of the daily routine, practiced in a variety of keys.

EXAMPLE 8.8.

EXAMPLE 8.9.

The alveolar [r] is useful in furthering tongue freedom. In all but pop vocal idioms, the retroflex American or midwestern [r] is to be shunned. However, in some instances where American song literature requires colloquialism (Charles Ives, for example), the midwestern [r] may be permissible.

As earlier noted, in classical vocalism the phoneme [r] comes in two forms: the single-flipped [r] and the extended tongue-point trill (the rolled r). Occasionally a singer claims she can neither flip nor roll the consonant [r]. She may be convinced that her tongue is too long, too short, too skinny, or too fat to allow her to do so. This is almost never the case. (In rare instances, a frenectomy [severing of the ligament that attaches the frontal body of the tongue to the floor of the mouth] is necessary, but this has often been attended to in early infancy.) Lethargic tongue action can almost always be attributed to regional or familial speech habits that place the tongue in transitional phonetic positions.

The singer who believes she cannot produce the single-flipped [r] can substitute a quickly executed American alveolar [d] (formed with the tip of the tongue) in its place. She sings swiftly-moving syllabic patterns that alternate the [d] and the single-flipped [r], as in *ma-dia, ma-ria, ma-dia, ma-ria* (ex. 8.8). Both "words" should sound the same.

The American pronunciation of the word "body" gives the pronunciation (including the single-flipped [r]) of the Italian city Bari (ex. 8.9).

An amusing exercise borrowed from speech therapy is often successful in producing greater tongue agility for the singer who labors under sluggish tongue action. Although the English phrase "pot-a-tea" does not in itself produce the tongue roll, its rapid repetition and immediate alternation with the Italian "parti" can produce favorable results. Other swiftly executed phrases such as "put-it-out" (purraut) and "get-it-out" (ghuerraut) can serve in similar fashion (see 8.10–8.11) for rolled r.

These simple exercises, persistently drilled over a period of weeks (in some cases, months may be required), can help the singer to find increased articulatory flexibility of the tongue.

EXAMPLE 8.10.

"pot - a - tea," "par - ti,"   "pot - a - tea," "par - ti,"   "pot - a - tea," "par - ti"

EXAMPLE 8.11.

"get - it - out," "grrout,"   "get - it - out," "grrout,"   "get - it - out," "grrout"

EXAMPLE 8.12.

a. [ki - ke,   ki - ke,   ki - ke, ki - ke, ki - ke, ki - ke,   ki]
b. [ko - ka,   ko - ka,   ko - ka, ko - ka, ko - ka, ko - ka,   ko]

Another consonant pair proves of value in adjusting the resonator tract: the velar voiced-unvoiced combination [g–k]. In the case of either consonant, the mouth is excluded as a resonator, because the tongue and the velum are in contact. During the production of [g], which is voiced, the singer is aware of a subglottic response, but sound does not emerge by way of mouth or nose until a vowel follows. The sudden release of the linguavelar closure that produces the consonant [g] gives a sense of directness to the onset of the vowel.

The role of pilot consonant played by the unvoiced consonant [k] deserves special attention (ex. 8.12). Awareness of the physical formation of the phoneme [k]—exclusion of the buccal cavity—heightens recognition of linguavelar closure, because neither breath nor tone can have emission until some subsequent phonetic gesture has released the point of occlusion.

Because [k] prohibits both airflow and phonation, it induces a vividly perceived contact among muscles of the anterolateral abdominal wall, as is the case with the nasal continuant [m]. Patterns that make use of [k] as a pilot consonant leading to subsequent vowels help heighten a singer's consciousness of both the *appoggio* and the natural adjustment of the resonator tract for ensuing vowels.

Following the brief moment of closure produced by contact between tongue and velum with [k], the occluded portion of the vocal tract is reconnected for the ensuing vowel; the velum automatically assumes the proper level of elevation while the tongue spontaneously finds the appropriate position for the vowel to be enunciated.

EXAMPLE 8.13.

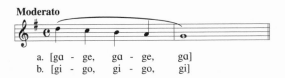

This procedure removes the need for attempted localized elevation of the faucial arch and the velum, and makes unnecessary the search for spaciousness in the velopharyngeal region. Phonetic proficiency replaces the necessity to consciously lift and hold the soft palate.

As mentioned earlier, analogous use can be made of [g] as a pilot onset consonant. For some singers, it is as beneficial to preface vowels with [g] as with [k] (see ex. 8.13).

Many techniques of singing that advocate conscious velar elevation and that aim for enlargement in the region of the soft palate are built on an assumption that it should be possible to distend the pharyngeal wall beyond the confines of Passavant's ridge. (Passavant's ridge is the soft cushion of fibers that covers the bony structure of the skull opposite the velar area; it is part of the superior constrictor muscle located at the juncture of the nasopharynx and the oropharynx, where an arching velum closes off the nasopharynx from the buccal cavity [see fig. 7.1].) It is not physiologically possible to create a resonating "dome" in the velar region of the pharynx. The singer who thinks she is making space in the nasal pharynx, or in the oropharynx, is actually spreading and tensing the faucial muscles (the palatoglossal and the palatopharyngeal muscular pillars attached to the walls of the pharynx and to the lateral base of the tongue). She is unintentionally inducing stress in the suspensory musculature of the larynx and among muscle groups in the submandibular (immediately beneath the jaw) region.

For singers who have a problem producing clean, nonbreathy or nonpressed onsets, the stop consonants [k] and [g] can be highly beneficial. The onset exercises described in chapter 3 may be prefaced by [k] and [g]. As initiators of sung phonation, these phonemes prohibit excessive emission of airflow. It should be kept in mind that breath is already present in the trachea, immediately available for instantaneous use; air cannot be sent to the larynx from some location in the lower abdomen. Consonants [k] and [g] make this manifest.

A further device for achieving tongue flexibility and articulatory precision consists of combining the stop linguavelar consonants [g] and [k] with the flipped consonants [r] and [l], followed by a vowel. This consonantal intermingling tends to reestablish the natural process of vocal-tract response to the laryngeally generated vowel (ex. 8.14).

EXAMPLE 8.14.

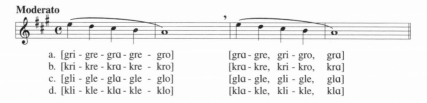

```
a. [gri - gre - gra - gre - gro]     [gra - gre, gri - gro,   gra]
b. [kri - kre - kra - kre - kro]     [kra - kre, kri - kro,   kra]
c. [gli - gle - gla - gle - glo]     [gla - gle, gli - gle,   gla]
d. [kli - kle - kla - kle - klo]     [kla - kle, kli - kle,   kla]
```

EXAMPLE 8.15.

```
a. [si  -  se,   sa  -  se,    so]
b. [zi  -  ze,   za  -  ze,    zo]
```

EXAMPLE 8.16.

```
a. [sle - sla, sle - sla - sle]    [zre - zra, zre, zra,   zre]    [sla - zra, sla - zra - sla]
b. [slo - sla, slo - sla - slo]    [zro - zra, zro, zra,   zro]    [zli - sre, zla - sro - zli]
```

The unvoiced-voiced [s] and [z] sibilant pair can be salutary in directing the singer to proper tongue postures, that is, in engaging the tongue with the inner surface of the lower front teeth while allowing the body of the tongue to elevate or to flatten in response to front or back vowel formations (ex. 8.15).

Both [s] and [z] can be favorably combined with the alveolar [r] and [l] to further tongue flexibility and elicit clean enunciation (ex. 8.16). At first blush, it may appear that the resulting consonantal clusters are artificial, but it should be recognized that phrases such as "is risen" and "is late" or "this room" and "this lyre" use similar phonetic combinations. Singers interested in perfecting articulatory ease find these exercises a pleasure.

Equally fruitful in consonantal piloting for a following vowel is the English language [d–t] pair (more dental than alveolar in the Romance languages), during which the tongue apex is in light contact with the alveolar ridge (ex. 8.17). Especially in the soprano *passaggio* region, if the onset on a vowel lacks freedom, it is good practice to preface it with one or the other member of this lingua-alveolar consonant pair. Whenever an onset in the literature begins nonvibrantly or torpidly, momentary insertion of a light [t] or [d] may solve the problem. Then return to the original text.

EXAMPLE 8.17.

a. [dɑ - de, dɑ - de,   dɑ - de, dɑ]   [drɑ - dre, drɑ - dre,   drɑ - dre, drɑ]
b. [tɑ - te, tɑ - te,   tɑ - te, tɑ]   [trɑ - tre, trɑ - tre,   trɑ - tre, trɑ]

For some performers freedom is momentarily hampered by subglottic sensations associated with the consonants [d] and [g]. To avoid that annoyance, during practice sessions the singer may first insert an aspirated [h] or a nasal [m] before the vowel. Then the original syllable is sung again, generally with increased freedom. But there is an inherent danger in this practice. Some singers become unconsciously dependent on phonetic crutches during performance, preceding syllables that begin with the subglottic consonants [d] and [g] with an [h] or an [m]: "[h]dal," "[m]day," "[h] gay," and "[m]God." Generally, making the singer aware of the phonetic formations of [d] and [g] and alerting the ear to unwarranted consonantal insertions will correct the habit.

In summation, a singer should experiment in a systematic way with series of consonants as onset-pilot devices to discover which induce freer vocalism in the subsequent phrase. Because of their physiologic formation and their acoustic nature, both nasals and nonnasals can be major devices for achieving good resonance balancing in the singing voice.

Musical patterns for the consonantal combinations suggested above can be whatever the singer and teacher wish to contrive. Basic patterns such as 1–2–3–2–1, 5–4–3–2–1, 1–3–5–3–1, 1–3–5–8–5–3–1, and 8–5–3–1 are typical; there is no magic in pitch formulae themselves. Adherence to the principle of efficient phonetic production is the aim of this family of exercises.

9

The Sostenuto Factor

The two poles of bel canto writing are well illustrated in the cavatina/cabaletta of the opera scena. This musical form traditionally consists of a recitative, a sustained aria, and a swiftly moving pyrotechnical second aria, sometimes with another recitative inserted between the two arias. (The cabaletta following the solo aria may also be found in duet form.) Beginning in the late eighteenth century and continuing through Verdi, the scena form flourished in opera, increasingly replacing the da capo aria so characteristic of Handel and his contemporaries. In part, the substitution of the duo aria (cavatina/cabaletta) for the da capo framework came in answer to the growing demand for dramatic evolution of plot and character. No longer did textual and musical repetitions of the ABA form seem adequate for moving the drama forward.

But there is a more compelling explanation: as solo vocal virtuosity began to reach new heights in the final decades of the eighteenth century—spilling over into the nineteenth—the display of technical skill became an end itself. Composers reacted to the technical prowess of premier singers, and opera audiences demanded increased demonstration of pyrotechnical vocal feats. The ability to sustain and to move the voice in all ranges became essential components of professional vocalism.

In line with a systematic presentation of vocal technique, the agility factor was introduced early in this book. Before extensive sostenuto passages can be successfully negotiated, the soprano (like singers of all vocal categories) must be able to move her voice freely. The vocal literature itself seldom deals separately with these two facets, because the two poles of bel canto (agility and sostenuto) are complementary. Yet it is necessary to bypass most sostenuto aspects in early considerations of breath management, agility, vowel differentiation, and resonance balancing, because sostenuto is an advanced technical component of the singing art, to which we now turn our attention.

The sustained section of the scena often presents a daunting task even for established professionals. For example, most Countesses experience relief when they leave behind the long lines of the cavatina *"Dove sono"* (*Le nozze di Figaro*, Mozart) for the

EXAMPLE 9.1.

subsequent cabaletta. Most Donna Annas, as well, visibly unwind a bit when they conclude the sustained "*Non mi dir*" at "se di duol non vuoi ch'io mora!, non ch'io mora!"), finding liberation in the melismatic running of the allegretto moderato at "Forse, forse un giorno il cielo ancora sentirà pietà di me!" If the soprano does not have the ability to cope with the melismatic second half of the aria, it is doubtful that she will have sufficient freedom to successfully sustain the sostenuto first half.

The best way to approach sostenuto technique is not to sing over and over songs and arias that have long phrases in the hope of building up sufficient stamina to eventually manage them. Rather, the same principle underlying the exercises constructed on phrases of both short and moderate duration encountered in chapter 4 needs to be applied to technical work on the sustained passages found in the literature: breath renewal is incorporated into the release, and the next onset takes place within the same quiet thoracic-cage posture. In so doing, *appoggio* reliability for sustained singing is developed. As a further maneuver, sostenuto passages are then sandwiched in between brief agility and onset patterns. The following group of exercises is appropriate for all categories of soprano.

An example of how agility, sostenuto, and onset can be combined within a single vocalise is found in example 9.1. The pattern should progress sequentially through several keys, but not beyond the singer's comfortable pitch range. Then follows an elongation of the sostenuto portion, as in example 9.2. A further extension of the sustained portion appears in example 9.3.

Example 9.4 starts in middle voice. The key of A♭ makes a logical beginning for the soubrette, the key of G for the lyric, and F♯ or F for the dramatic (F or E for the mezzo-soprano). The pattern ought to be extended by semitones through the *secondo passaggio* (see chapter 2 for a discussion of the *passaggi*). The exercise then descends by semitone tonalities to lower voice. The entire pattern should be sung on a single front vowel, preferably [e] or [ɛ], then on a single back vowel, preferably [ɔ] or [o].

Next, the sequence of vowels should shift from front to back vowel or back to front (depending on which vowel began the series), continuing to the conclusion of the phrase. Other vowel changes may be added. Example 9.4 is sung at a walking tempo, without dragging. As with many sostenuto exercises, it serves as a registration vocalise as well.

EXAMPLE 9.2.

EXAMPLE 9.3.

EXAMPLE 9.4.

EXAMPLE 9.5.

The notation pattern of example 9.4 is then reversed (ex. 9.5). It may begin in upper middle voice and descend to lower middle voice. A single front vowel is sung; then the exercise is repeated on a back vowel. Immediately thereafter, on the third note of each phrase, a front vowel is substituted for the back vowel, with the substituted vowel continuing through the phrase. A front vowel, when it has introduced the sequence, then shifts to the back vowel on the third note of each pattern, and this alternation continues throughout the phrase.

Example 9.6 has a long history as a sostenuto vocalise. It was championed by both Maestro Mario Basiola and Maestro Luigi Ricci in the mid-twentieth century as a

EXAMPLE 9.6.

        a. [i_____]   [e]   [ɑ_____]   [e]   [i]
        b. [ɑ_____]   [e]   [e_____]   [e]   [ɑ]

EXAMPLE 9.7.

        a. [i_____] [e_____] [ɑ]   [i_____] [e_____] [ɑ]
        b. [ɑ_____] [e_____] [i]   [ɑ_____] [e_____] [i]

major technical device of the Cotogni-Lamperti school for building sostenuto stamina in the mature voice: *con quest' esercizio si fa la voce* ("with this exercise you build the voice"). Based on the triad, it should be sung slowly; breath renewal is rhythmically paced.

Most sopranos will want to begin in the key of $E^\flat$ (at $E^\flat_4$), progress by semitones to higher tonalities, and arrive at the key of F (F_5) so that C_6 (high C) becomes the top note of the triad. Then, by semitone, the singer descends to lower middle voice, terminating the vocalise at F_4 in the key of F. In accordance with the system of vocalization prominent in the historic Italian school, lateral and rounded vowels alternately begin the exercise, so that one time a front vowel is on the fifth note of the scale, the next time a back vowel. This exercise should not be undertaken until breath management, laryngeal freedom, and resonance balance have become secure. As an essential part of the daily vocal routine of a maturing technique, it should be executed in its entirety throughout a singer's performable range.

Another major sostenuto vocalise that has value for the advanced singer (but not for beginners of any age) is based on slow arpeggiation that ascends on the tonic major chord and descends on the seventh chord (exercise 9.7). For most lyric sopranos and soubrettes this exercise should begin in the key of F (at F_4) and progress upward chromatically so that C_6 becomes the upper note, then return by semitone to the lower octave. The dramatic soprano may wish to begin in the key of $E^\flat$ (at $E^\flat_4$), extending the vocalise upward by semitone, the uppermost note terminating at $B^\flat_5$. Then she should descend by way of chromatic tonalities to the original octave. Vowel alternation follows the principle of juxtaposition of front and back vowels as in example 9.6.

After singing a sostenuto exercise, the soprano should return to one of the quickly moving agility patterns in chapter 5. Although it is unwise to do both the heavy-duty

EXAMPLE 9.8.

Langsam und leise

Im - mer lei - ser wird mein Schlum - mer   nur wie Schlei - er liegt mein

Kum - mer   zit - ternd ü - ber mir___   ü - ber   mir.___

EXAMPLE 9.9.

Zart

Wie Me - lo - di - en___ zieht es mir lei - se durch den Sinn,   wie

Früh - lings-blu - men blüht es, und schwebt wie Duft da - hin   und

schwebt   wie Duft   da - hin.

sostenuto vocalises of examples 9.6 and 9.7 during a single practice session, one of them ought to be chosen for inclusion in the daily routine.

A vast number of demanding *sostenuto* exercises can be selected from the soprano literature itself. For young sopranos, the opening passage of Gluck's familiar "*O del mio dolce ardor*" offers an excellent excerptable vocalise. Sequentially sung in near keys, it drills the coordination between *appoggio* retention and breath renewal, which is the essence of sostenuto singing.

Singing repeatedly through Handel's "*O Sleep! Why Dost Thou Leave Me*" is not an efficient way for a young soprano to master sostenuto. Repeating just the opening phrases in neighboring keys produces far better results. Based on the coordination achieved through repetition of the excerpted vocalise, remaining phrases of the aria can gradually be added.

Johannes Brahms, with his penchant for flowing vocal lines that delay final resolution, is an inexhaustible treasure of passages to be taken out of context for use as vocalises. The opening phrases of "*Immer leiser wird mein Schlummer*," in transposition for high voice, are an example (ex. 9.8). This is equally the case with "*Wie Melodien zieht es mir*." The beginning melodic phrases should be sung in several progressively higher tonalities (ex. 9.9).

Example 9.10.

Ne ja-mais la voir ni l'en - ten - dre, Ne ja-mais tout haut la nom - mer,

Example 9.11.

Non mi____ dir,____bell' i - dol mi - o

che son i - o cru - del____ con te,

Especially useful for lyric soprano voices as literature excerpts are phrases from "*Soupir*," a mélodie by Duparc. The first phrase begins in upper middle voice, then descends to lower middle voice; the second phrase mirrors the shape of the first but lies a third higher (ex. 9.10). These two phrases can profitably be repeated several times in the original key as a sequential exercise, then transposed upward and downward.

No better sostenuto exercise could be devised for the ample lyric soprano or dramatic soprano voice (not for the soubrette) than the opening phrases of Donna Anna's "*Non mi dir*" (*Don Giovanni*, Mozart), as in example 9.11. As a practice measure, it is advisable to sing as vocalises a few phrases from the aria, rather than to sing through the entire lengthy, sustained piece. Excerpted phrases are to be sung in near-key sequences, breath renewal being rhythmically paced between tonalities. The several patterns of the examples, when routined in a systematic fashion, bring stability to subsequent cumulative phrases. One may also begin with later, non-cumulative phrases, carefully determining breath pacing and vowel definition for each of them and gradually adding a phrase or two each day, then reversing the process by working backward to the beginning of the aria.

Many motifs can be selected from the literature to serve as vocalization excerpts, but these patterns from readily available sources prove particularly beneficial. Not only do such exercises supply practical vocalization material for sopranos, they transplant technical work into musical and emotive contexts. They attest that it is not possible to separate technique from musicianly concerns.

10

Soprano Vocal Registration and
Vowel Modification (Aggiustamento)

As indicated in chapter 2, the long soprano middle voice typically extends from $E\flat_4$ to $F\sharp_5$, with $C\sharp_5$ the dividing midpoint between the lower middle and upper middle ranges. In light soubrette voices, the long middle register is negotiated from bottom to top, and from top to bottom, with little awareness of a dividing point between the lower middle and upper middle segments or of the need to alter breath energy to accommodate ascending pitch. A soubrette soprano inflects her speech and laughter to higher pitch levels than does the soprano with a more sizable instrument. Sopranos with instruments of lyric proportions often find that if they do not increase breath energy around $C\sharp_5$, vocal timbre will become weak or unstable. Sopranos of more substantial vocal proportions often experience this mid-range registration event around C_5. Still larger soprano voices may be aware of such an occurrence between lower middle and upper middle voice as early as B_4. These phenomena, occurring midway in the soprano's long middle range, correlate with the upper limit of the singer's occasional speech-inflection range. Because the soprano is entering a pitch region not generally used during normal intensity levels of speech, additional breath energy (an increase in *appoggio*) is demanded of her.

It has been noted that registration sensations experienced by women during singing correspond to regions of the musical scale; in traditional pedagogic language they are designated as "chest," "mixed," and "head." (Chapter 2 considered sensation awareness at pivotal register points as an assist in determining voice categorization.) In order to avoid the erroneous notion that tone is placed in physical locations, it is useful to designate these regions "low voice," "middle voice," and "upper voice." Yet head (*voix de tête, voce di testa, Kopfstimme*), mixed (*voix mixte, voce mista, gemischte Stimme*), and chest (*voix de poitrine, voce di petto, Bruststimme*) are expressions imbedded in the language of international pedagogy. In addition, when dealing with the several timbre possibilities of the female low voice, traditional designations are almost unavoidable. The generic (soubrette through lyric) soprano voice may be described as follows:

1. low range, from G_3 to $E^\flat_4$ (chest);
2. middle range, from $E^\flat_4$ to $F^\sharp_5$ (mixed), subdivided into lower middle, from $E^\flat_4$ to $C^\sharp_5$, and upper middle, from $C^\sharp_5$ to $F^\sharp_5$ (mixed);
3. upper range, from $F^\sharp_5$ to C_6 or $C^\sharp_6$ (head); and
4. flageolet range, from around D_6 or $D^\sharp_6$ to the highest negotiable pitches.

Sections of this chapter will be devoted to registration exercises for each of these traditionally designated regions of the soprano voice and for their integration into a unified scale.

Many faults in singing are traceable to deceptive theories as to the physical function of head voice and chest voice. Some registration theories incorrectly maintain that sopranos sing entirely in head except for an occasional excursion into chest voice in the lowest range, that the lower half of the negotiable range of the mezzo-soprano takes place all in chest, and that the contralto leaves chest only for her upper middle and upper ranges. (A similar theory suggests that basses, bass-baritones, and baritones sing almost entirely in chest up to F_4 [their high F], and that tenors sing the bottom half of their voices in chest and the upper half in head, or even in falsetto.) In these instances the location of sensations is mistaken for the physiological origin of vocal sound.

Although males normally speak in what is traditionally termed chest, most females inflect their speaking voices in both chest and head registers. Other females rely chiefly on one or the other of the two chief registers for most of the speech range. Speaking mostly in chest may be as true of the soprano (especially the dramatic) as of the mezzo-soprano.

In some pedagogies, the terms "light mechanism" and "heavy mechanism" designate the preponderance of either head or chest (see chapter 2). The problem with this terminology lies in its implication that the singing voice separately employs either one or the other of two disjunct physical functions. In fact, at both ascending and descending pitches, a graduated action among laryngeal muscle groups occurs. Especially during singing, register changes are generated in response to tonal concept, to airflow, and to laryngeal events that happen below the level of consciousness. (We recall that registration phenomena are not elicited by conscious localized laryngeal control, nor by the "placement" of tone in various regions of the head or chest.)

As was earlier seen (chapter 2) with regard to physical factors, registration occurrences differ widely between male and female voices. Although the disparity of registration within the comprehensive soprano category is much less than that between males and females, as has been indicated, register events do occur at slightly different locations in the scale among the soprano categories; it is a mistake to treat the *zona di passaggio* identically for all categories of soprano voice.

It was previously seen that as the fundamental (pitch) ascends, the contraction of the cricothyroid muscles tilts the thyroid and cricoid cartilages toward each other. (It is not the case, as was formerly assumed and is still maintained in some medical and voice pedagogy literatures, that only the thyroid cartilage moves.) These muscle engagements stretch the vocal folds. (See figure 2.5.) Vennard[1] terms this motion a "rocking" action. A second possible motion is termed "gliding." In gliding, through activation of the cricothyroid muscles, the lower horns of the thyroid cartilage are moved slightly forward from their point of articulation on the cricoid cartilage. Because at points in the mounting scale these cooperative actions (all below the level of consciousness) become more pronounced, and because they produce different acoustic results, the singer perceives them as events of registration. To review, these pivotal points correspond to pitch locations in the musical scale at which the rocking and gliding maneuvers of the cricoid and thyroid cartilages become more marked. The classification of voices described in chapter 1 is partly dependent on taking this information into account.

Clearly, elongation of the vocal folds and diminution of their mass as pitch ascends is partly the result of intrinsic and extrinsic laryngeal muscle action that produces movements of the thyroid and the cricoid cartilages. External-frame support of the larynx is essential to head and neck relationships. Therefore, the positions of the head and neck are vital to the successful progression from one voice register to another.

If the singer raises her head to accomplish intervallic leaps or in response to an ascending scale, the gliding and rocking actions needed to achieve pitch alteration are inhibited or even prohibited. Choreographing pitch elevation by raising either the head or the larynx, or both, induces register violation. During singing, the larynx should remain basically stable, supported by the coordinated neck musculature. (In the historic Italianate school, this external-frame support of the larynx is termed *appoggio della nucca*, the *nucca* being the nape of the neck.) Advocating that the head be raised in order to "free" the larynx is pernicious advice. One influential but physiologically insupportable American vocal pedagogy even recommends "the sword-swallowing position" as an ideal head and neck position for singing. This causes the innermost portion of the thyroarytenoids (the ligament of the vocal fold that forms the rim of the glottis) to be called on to assist excessively in changing pitch. Put another way, the vocal folds themselves attempt controls that place them in a greater state of tension than is necessary. Register violation (retention of a particular function beyond its normal location in a region of the scale) results in thin timbre or, alternatively, in an audible break.

No matter how limited the interval, unskillful sopranos tend to elevate chin and head for upwardly moving pitch changes. Intervals that approach or go beyond registration pivotal points are especially susceptible to pitch choreography.

Another common error is for the lyric soprano to depress her head for pitches below the lower *passaggio* ($E\flat_4$), then to elevate her head for those near or above the upper *passaggio* ($F\sharp_5$). Sometimes even the midpoint in the long middle register ($C\sharp_5$)

will tempt the singer to raise or to lower her head, thereby altering external-frame support for the larynx. It must be reiterated that when either the head or the larynx is elevated, the gliding and rocking actions of the laryngeal cartilages cannot take place freely; timbre at the registration points is altered, and it becomes more difficult to achieve an even scale.

It is true that changing the position of the head when in the lower and middle ranges produces a less drastic loss in timbre than is the case in the upper middle and upper ranges. Yet lowering the chin to produce low pitches is as devastating to register unification as is raising the chin for high notes. After having established technical habits that produce a stable laryngeal position, the soprano in middle register may with impunity occasionally "sing to the balcony," or she may lower her head for dramatic effect. However, when head elevation for a mounting or a descending pitch is embedded in the technique, a segmented scale will result; harmonic components of the spectrum cannot be kept in balance.

Some investigators have speculated that in soprano extreme upper range—as in flageolet production—elevating the larynx shortens the distance of the vocal tract from the glottis to the velum, making additional high pitches possible. Overlooked is the distinctly unfavorable shrill resonance imbalance that results from this violation of efficient laryngeal action. Although never rigidly maintained, laryngeal position should always remain stable.

In some pedagogies, the *passaggi* points are called "lifts of the breath." Advocates of this nomenclature speak of "first" and "second" lifts. In North America, this terminology stems from Herbert Witherspoon, most probably adapted from the *passaggi* teachings of G. B. Lamperti and Cotogni. This is because additional *appoggio* action in the anterior-lateral-dorsal region of the torso ensures appropriate aerodynamic response to the laryngeal events involved in register change. However, Witherspoon's approach is often misinterpreted, with singers "lifting" inward and upward on the abdominal wall at registration points. The term *appoggio* should replace the easily misunderstood "lift."

It has been repeatedly stressed that the voice is an aerodynamic/myoelastic instrument—that is, movement of air sets the vocal folds into vibration. Breath energy, gradually increasing as pitch and intensity rise, and vocal fold closure responding to it become more marked at *passaggio* points. That means an increase in *appoggio* action is necessary, especially at the *secondo passaggio*, and it should not be negated by inward abdominal thrusting,

It is the singer's task to increase breath energy without unduly increasing subglottic pressure (see chapter 4). It has been a premise of this book that any increase in breath energy must be accomplished by maintaining the dynamic antagonism among the muscles of the abdominal and lower back regions. Especially at the pivotal registration points, *appoggio* breath management modifies the normal increase in subglottic pressure and airflow that are essential to the production of pitches that lie in the *passaggio* zone.

No singer while singing sustained phrases can stay in exactly the same inspiratory position that was established at the moment of breath renewal. However, if the singer has developed the abdominal musculature that permits extended maintenance of the *appoggio*, she will be able to remain in the initial inspiratory position longer than she could during a normal breath cycle. She counteracts the tendency for the sternum to fall and the ribcage to collapse, and she delays the recoil action of the lungs. This coordination is required above all when voice registration tasks are encountered. Four physical parameters intertwine in the accomplishment of the breath management essential to an even vocal registration:

1. the sternum remains at a comfortably elevated position throughout the breath cycle,
2. the ribcage is fully expanded, neither rising nor falling at inhalation or during the execution of the phrase,
3. the diaphragm remains as long as possible at its lowest position, and
4. the normal rate of lung recoil is retarded.

It is precisely at the *passaggio* points where the unskillful soprano often allows chest displacement to occur. During a breath cycle that is adequate for speech, shortly after the inspiratory gesture is completed, the sternum begins to lower, the cage moves inward, and the diaphragm rapidly ascends. As a result of this normal expiratory gesture, the volume of air in the lung is quickly depleted. In singing, counteracting this collapse is essential to the accomplishment of an evenly registered scale. In all voices there is a direct correspondence between registration and resonance balancing. A uniformly resonant timbre is not possible unless breath energy (breath management, best accomplished by the *appoggio*) is adjusted to match voice registration requirements.

Because so much of the literature for all kinds of soprano lies within the long middle-voice register, both song and opera sources are replete with excerptable registration exercises.

As when working on all registers of the soprano voice, it is to Mozart that one can profitably turn when working on establishing uniform middle-range registration. With good reason, "*Ridente la calma*" has long been a staple in the study of resonance balancing for the soprano middle voice. The passage "Tu vieni frattanto a stringer, mio bene, le dolci catene sì grate al mio cor" (ex. 10.1) lies almost entirely in the upper middle range, with an occasional excursion into the region of the *secondo passaggio*. It should be sung

1. on a single vowel selected from the lateral vowel series,
2. on a single vowel from the rounded vowel series,
3. on the vowels inherent in the text, minus the consonants, and finally,
4. with the text.

At the intervallic leap of the seventh on the syllable *string-* of *stringer* there must be an increase in breath energy as the phrase enters the *zona di passaggio*. Soon there-

EXAMPLE 10.1.

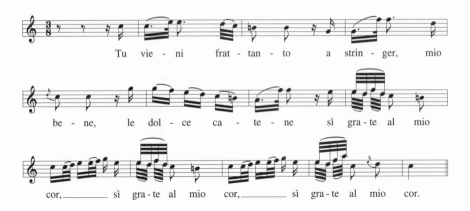

Tu vie - ni frat - tan - to a strin - ger, mio
be - ne, le dol - ce ca - te - ne sì gra - te al mio
cor,_____ sì gra - te al mio cor,_____ sì gra - te al mio cor.

after, the section beginning on G₅ with "*le dolci catene*" clearly requires more energy than it would if it began an octave lower. Such increase in breath energy is not achieved by pulling inward on the abdomen nor by pushing outward, but by maintaining dynamic muscle equilibrium in the anterior and lateral abdominal and lower dorsal regions.

In this miniature aria, Mozart devises a superb study in variations of energy distribution in the *zona di passaggio* through his three settings of the text "*sì grate al mio cor.*" The singer who pushes in and out on her abdominal wall in order to articulate rising and falling pitches of the passage will here readily see the fallacy of that approach. Stability of the torso (described above) facilitates proper dynamic breath management. The well-disposed phrases of "*Ridente la calma*" can then be shaped and tapered without loss of legato.

Some passages that ideally serve the soubrette or light soprano as practical vocalization exercises for achieving consistent timbre in middle voice come from the popular "*In uomini, in soldati*" (*Così fan tutte*, Mozart). In its original key, the syllabically set and quickly moving passage beginning "Di pasta simile son tutti quanti" (ex. 10.2) lies in a convenient range. It also proves fruitful when transposed to several near tonalities, particularly in focusing on timbre consistency during the descent from upper middle to lower middle ranges. During the octave leaps, the abdominal wall remains *appoggiato*, and the mouth adjusts flexibly.

Bellini, intensely alert to emotive potentials inherent in the colors of soprano voice registers, is another of the great voice teachers of all time. The *arioso* section of the *recitativo accompagnato* beginning with "Ardo . . . una vampa, un foco tutta mi strugge," and the aria "*O quante volte*" (*I Capuleti e i Montecchi*) that follows it, serve as a combined reservoir of outstanding exercises in vocal registration. Together, the already-cited beginning—"Eccomi in lieta vesta"—of the *recitativo accompagnato*

EXAMPLE 10.2.

Di pa-sta si-mi-le son tut-ti quan-ti, son tut-ti quan-ti: le fron-de mo - bi-li, l'aure in-co - stan - ti han più de - gli uo-mi - ni sta-bi-li - tà.

(see ex. 4.14), the arioso, and the aria itself call for the chief components of stabilized vocal technique:

1. precise onset, release, and renewal of the breath,
2. clean vowel differentiation,
3. graduated vowel modification,
4. supple agility,
5. fluent sostenuto,
6. subtle dynamic control,
7. equalized resonance balance within the even scale, and
8. expressive phrase sculpturing and pacing.

With its graciously flowing cantilena, both the recitative and the aria serve as vehicles for training all soprano voice categories not only in registration but in the technical and musical facets of bel canto. This beautifully constructed composition should be a soprano's *vade mecum*. The lyric soprano would do well to use portions of the entire composition as road maps for journeys in daily vocalization.

All categories of soprano voice, but especially the light lyric soprano, will find Donizetti to be a storehouse of material for the development of technical and musical adroitness. No better pattern for exercising upper-middle-voice registration and resonance balancing has been devised than the passage "Prendi, per me sei libero; resta nel suol natio; non v'ha destin sì rio, che non si cangi un dì, resta. Qui, dove tutti t'amano, saggio, amoroso, onesto" from the *L'elisir d'amore* aria. As a vocalise, each amiable segment incorporates vowel differentiation, silent breath renewal, and chiaroscuro resonance balancing. Every phrase of the aria has its own musical life, but the shapes and trajectories of each do not interrupt overall unity.

In Marzelline's "*O wär ich schon mit dir vereint*" (*Fidelio*), Beethoven proves himself well versed in soprano middle-voice registration practices. An especially adaptable passage for excerpting begins at the poco più allegro with "Die Hoffnung schon erfüllt die Brust mit unaussprechlich süsser Lust, wie glücklich will ich werden!" This

aria demands in middle register what many internationally oriented German peda-
gogues rightly describe as an *ausgeglichene Stimme* (ironed-out voice). With its rapid
movement, the suggested passage contrasts well with middle-voice sostenuto studies.

For the lyric soprano, an ideal vocalise comes from the opening phrases of "*St.
Ita's Vision*" (*Songs of Hermitage*, Barber): "'I will take nothing from my Lord,' said
she, 'unless He gives me His Son from Heaven, In the form of a Baby that I may nurse
Him.' So that Christ came down to her in the form of a Baby—and then she said."
These six measures of recitative should be sung sequentially in several near tonalities.
The technical aim of the exercise is to retain timbre consistency throughout while
shifting freely over upper middle and lower middle ranges.

For the large soprano instrument it would be difficult to find passages better
suited for establishing timbre unification in sustained middle voice than those in the
Contessa's cavatina "*Dove sono*" (*Le nozze di Figaro*, Mozart). The fifteen-measure
setting of the text "Dove sono i bei momenti, di dolcezza e di piacer, dove andaro
i giuramenti di quel labbro menzogner!" should be sung as an exercise, repeated
several times in sequence with special attention directed to constancy of vibrancy
(perceived as timbre enhancement, not as pitch variation, i.e., no straight-toning),
exactitude of vowel differentiation, presence of the *chiaroscuro*, and silent breath renewal. These elements are combined within an overall arching, gracious phrase shape.

Robert Schumann was fully aware of the technical and artistic accomplishments
of the major singing artists of his day. In addition to achieving a new form of lyric
declamation (in which word inflection often determines the shape of the vocal line
and of rhythm) in such early cycles as *Dichterliebe* and *Frauenliebe und -leben*, Schumann made full use of a palette dependent on voice registration colors, particularly in his later period. His "*Kennst du das Land*," set in June of 1849, offers a study
in middle voice registration. Sopranos of all categories (except perhaps the
soubrette) can use Schumann's soulful setting of Goethe's magnificent text as an exercise for middle-voice registration equalization and as a study in exactitude of vowel
definition and phonetic articulation in sung German:

> Kennst du das Land, wo die Zitronen blühn,
> Im dunkeln Laub die Gold-Orangen glühn,
> Ein sanfter Wind vom blauen Himmel weht,
> die Myrte still und hoch der Lorbeer steht?
> Kennst du es wohl?
> Dahin! dahin
> Möcht ich mit dir, o mein Geliebter, ziehn.

By isolating these and similar passages as vocalises, the singer concentrates on
timbre relationships among shifting intervals and alternating vowels. Detaching such
segments for technical attention sharpens awareness of timbre constancy and secures
register unification for future performance.

EXAMPLE 10.3.

Exercises of brief duration are useful in systematically directing the singer's attention to consistency of timbre regardless of registration pivotal points. Example 10.3 lodges chiefly in upper middle voice, then descends to lower middle voice. The series should be sung

1. on a lateral vowel,
2. on a rounded vowel, and then
3. with a change of vowels on each subsequent phrase.

Other registration exercises direct attention to the subtle adjustments in breath energy required as pitch mounts from lower middle to upper middle voice. When singing upward intervals, most sopranos need to be aware of an increase in breath energy (and to be reminded not to raise the larynx).

The gradual mouth opening (*aggiustamento*) that should take place as pitch ascends must be systematically drilled. This *aggiustamento* follows a natural vowel-modification process (see figure 10.1) because as the mouth opens to accommodate ascending pitch, the vowel tends to migrate to a neighboring vowel:

[i] to [ɪ],
[ɪ] to [e],
[e] to [ɛ],
[ɛ] to [ɑ],
[ɑ] to [ɔ],
[ɔ] to [o],
[o] to [ʊ],
[ʊ] to [u].

This process is a subtle migration of the vowel series toward neutralization.

It is not possible to build a vowel-modification chart that is exact for every voice. Shadings of vowel modification must be tailored to the individual instrument, male or female. There should be no sudden loss of vowel recognition at *passaggi* points. In *aggiustamento*, front vowels must gradually modify toward the neutral center. As the upper *passaggio* is approached this modification becomes more pronounced, but above all, the neutralization of all vowels in the direction of [ə] ("uh") as soon

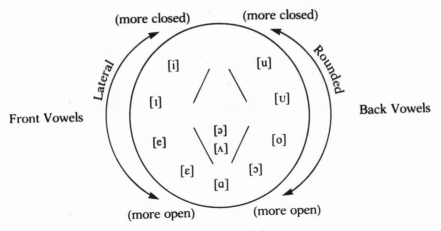

FIGURE 10.1. *Vowel modification* (aggiustamento) *chart*

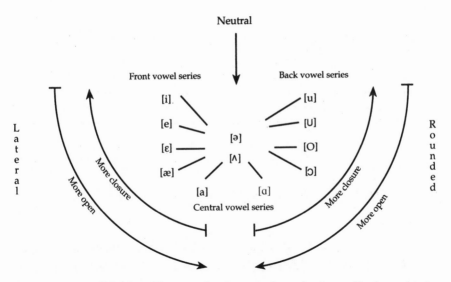

FIGURE 10.2. *Modification of front vowel series, central vowel series, and back vowel series.*

as the upper *passaggio* ($F^\sharp_5$–G_5) is passed is to be strenuously avoided. In order to minimize the conjoining of high harmonic partials and high pitch, the front vowels must modify in the direction of the neutral center; the back vowels may need more closure (see fig. 10.2), also a process of neutralization.

A sequence of [i–e–ɑ–o–u], sung on the same pitch by an accomplished twenty-two-year-old lyric soprano, shows that although the number of harmonic partials lessens as pitch rises, when the vowels are appropriately modified, vowel integrity is still maintained (see fig. 10.3). The upper window displays spectral analysis of the

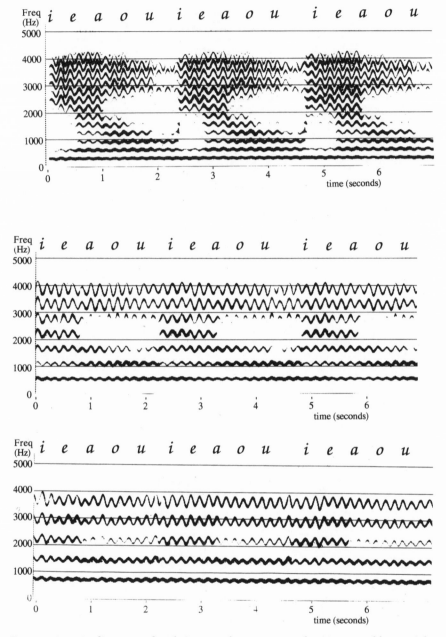

FIGURE 10.3. *An [i–e–a–o–u] real-time vowel sequence sung by a 22-year-old potential lyric soprano, indicating vowel definition at several frequencies: upper window: E♭₄; middle window: C♯₅; lower window: F♯₅. The horizontal axis represents time, the vertical axis, frequency (Hz). Wavy lines of the harmonic partials indicate vibrato. (Otto B. Schoepfle Vocal Arts Center, Oberlin Conservatory of Music, 1994)*

EXAMPLE 10.4.

EXAMPLE 10.5.

EXAMPLE 10.6.

vowel sequence at E♭$_4$ (the lower *passaggio* pivotal note), here sung in head, the middle window that of C♯$_5$ (the mid-register point between lower middle and upper middle voice); the lower window presents the same vowel series at F♯$_5$ (the lyric soprano upper *passaggio* pivotal point). The three spectrographic windows indicate that this young singer maintains the 4000 Hz ceiling on upper harmonics that is characteristic of premier sopranos.

Example 10.4 is designed to concentrate on the accomplishment of such *aggiustamento*. For the more dramatic soprano instrument, these events, both breath-management and vowel-modification maneuvers, occur a semitone or a whole tone lower. The complete exercise may be sung first on a single vowel, lateral or rounded, then with brief phrases alternating between lateral and rounded vowels.

The descending-octave pattern illustrated in example 10.5 is to be sung sequentially in several neighboring keys, first on a lateral, then on a rounded vowel. Shifts from lateral to rounded, then rounded to lateral, ought to be made with each ascending and descending octave pattern. The same is true of example 10.6, through its ascent from lower middle to upper middle voice, then its descent from upper middle to lower middle voice, touching each intervening pitch while maintaining the same chiaroscuro timbre. These patterns should be sung sequentially in neighboring tonalities at both higher and lower levels. Single vowels are used, alternating between lateral and rounded; a change from lateral to rounded, or the reverse, may occur on either the upper or the lower note of each pattern.

The intent with these intervallic exercises should be to retain uniform timbre in the singing voice despite leaps from lower middle to upper middle voice. Because the lower pitches are in speech-inflection range, buccal postures (mouth and jaw) will be closely akin to those at speech level. With upward intervallic leaps, particularly into the region of the *secondo passaggio* and above, the mouth will open (i.e., the jaw will lower) for pitches sung at higher levels. Yet during these intervallic skips, although the mouth opens more, the basic phonetic structure of the vowel, including the position of the lips and the zygomatic arch, is retained. At the return to the lower octave, the mouth resumes its speech posture. In summary, the following parameters ought to remain constant:

1. The mouth opens (jaw lowers) for ascending pitch, while other articulatory factors remain basically unaltered.
2. Lip shape (lateral, neutral, or rounded) stays nearly the same for the definition of a specific vowel, whether in speech mode or in singing mode, regardless of pitch level.
3. During singing, the tongue retains the vowel-defining postures of speech, even in intervallic leaps.
4. The zygomatic muscles remain slightly elevated, without smiling (no participation of the risorius muscles), even as the jaw lowers.
5. The velum and faucial arch retain the natural elevation that follows deep, silent inhalation, providing proper space between velum and larynx.
6. The larynx remains poised, neither rising nor falling, regardless of pitch change.

An opposing pedagogic viewpoint is that the jaw should remain in a hung position (inaccurately described as "relaxed"), retaining a basic low posture regardless of the vowel and pitch to be sung. That philosophy is in contrast to the changing acoustic events associated with energized phonation and laughter at high pitch in both speaking and singing. Opinion about the extent to which a vowel should be modified for the soprano voice in the mounting sung scale separates vocal pedagogies from each other. In some segments of central and northern European voice instruction, vowels typically are modified (through jaw lowering) at the middle-register subdivision point (around $C\sharp_5$), proceeding with marked neutralization above the *secondo passaggio* ($F\sharp_5$–G_5 for the lyric soprano). All vowels approach the neutral vowel "uh" [ə], or even the most back vowel "oo" [u]. This procedure is termed *Deckung* (covering). When vowels are thus early and uniformly modified, they tend to lose phonetic integrity and to be characterized by a lack of upper harmonic partials. In so doing, the chiaroscuro balance is destroyed, largely through loss of acoustic strength in the upper region of the spectrum; vowels are distorted into a uniform "tube tone," and clear diction is not achievable.

EXAMPLE 10.7.

EXAMPLE 10.8.

By contrast, the international school, based on a historic Italianate model, remains committed to vowel integrity as *aggiustamento* subtly achieves smooth register transition and an even scale. All vowel migration is a form of vowel neutralization, but modification must never occur abruptly. The avoidance of vowel modification will produce shrill, edgy timbre.

Example 10.7 is constructed on small intervals. In this case, the soprano begins in upper middle range and progresses downward, passing through middle voice and arriving at lower middle voice. She must be aware of timbre constancy throughout the descending figure. A series of several neighboring tonalities, both higher and lower, should be sung as well.

This exercise further drills the clean onset. It helps the singer recognize that the termination of each half note of every brief phrase incorporates silent breath renewal, followed immediately by the next vibrant onset. Further, the singer should consider this an exercise for enclosing short melodic fragments within longer phrase units, thereby producing an overall musical totality. Vowel changes that include patterns from lateral to rounded and from rounded to lateral should be employed.

Another helpful exercise for achieving register unification between upper middle and lower middle ranges for the soprano voice is found in example 10.8. It begins at the upper middle level, engages in descending intervals, then returns each time to upper middle voice. Several alternating vowel sequences may be introduced.

Productive technical study should never be separated from musical realization. Examples 10.3 through 10.8 help iron out registration timbres; through routining they encourage the singer to fuse phrase shaping, legato, and musical expression.

Vocalises have value only insofar as they are applicable to the literature. The purpose of integrating systematic *passaggio* exercises and literature examples is to remove technical study from a pedagogic vacuum and to give it performance enhancement. Vocalises ought to be alternated daily with selections from the indicated literature passages.

Bridging Middle and Upper Soprano Registers

From the literature can be selected passages that bridge middle and upper voice registers. Rather than to begin by singing the texts, it may be helpful to practice segments on single vowels or on the inherent vowels of a text, devoid of consonants. Then return to the complete text.

Mozart again proves an excellent voice teacher (ex. 10.9), which is illustrated by the phrase "ti vo' la fronte incoronar" (and its repetition) from Susanna's "*Deh, vieni, non tardar*" (*Le nozze di Figaro*). Mounting scales traverse the lower middle and upper middle ranges en route to upper voice, descend, and then re-ascend to speech-inflection range. On the first stepwise ascent on the syllables of *incoronar* (beginning at G_4 and ascending to A_5), the singer's mouth remains only slightly more open than it would be in speech until the syllable -*ro*-, at which point a gradual *aggiustamento* of the vowel begins: a subtle increase in mouth aperture and jaw lowering. On the syllable -*nar*, with its F_5–A_5–C_5–F_5–A_4 melodic excursion, the mouth will open considerably wider for A_5 (high A [880 Hz]), assume appropriate *aggiustamento* for the intervening pitches, and resume an articulatory posture close to that of speech for A_4 (440 Hz). In the second scale ascent on *incoronar*, from G_4 to F_5 (the sustained note on -*nar*), a gradual opening of the mouth will take place, but the mouth will not be opened as far on F_5 (-*nar*) as it was for high A. Then, in the third ascent on the same word (*incoronar*), a similar graduated modification occurs. By this means alone will vowel integrity and an even registration result. Any set postures of mouth and jaw that do not take into account pitch changes will cause vowel distortion and resonance imbalances. A mouth posture that is too narrow in upper middle range will cause shrillness; a mouth posture that is too open in lower middle range will cause muddiness of timbre. (It is an acoustic rule that the lateral position of the mouth uniformly strengthens upper harmonic partials, while the open-mouth position uniformly lowers harmonic partials.)

To serve the large soprano voice as a study in equalizing harmonic balance in middle voice with transition into the upper range, an ideal passage comes from the *Elijah* (Mendelssohn) in several phrases of the aria "*Hear Ye, Israel!*" (ex. 10.10). The

Example 10.9.

vie - ni! ti vo' la   fron - te in - co - ro - nar_____   di ro - se,   ti vo' la

fron - te in - co - ro - nar_____   in - co - ro - nar____   di ro - se!

EXAMPLE 10.10.

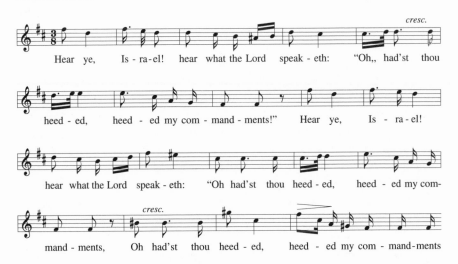

selected measures are useful in demonstrating relationships between vowel integrity and vowel modification (graduated mouth opening) in the lateral vowel [i] at several pitch levels. The opening "Hear ye" begins at F$\#_5$, the first note above the *secondo passaggio* for the spinto or dramatic soprano instrument. On the vowel [i] on this note, the mouth must open suitably in order to reduce the conjoining of high upper partials inherent in the vowel [i] with a relatively high fundamental pitch. The vowels [i] and [I] occur with considerable frequency within the syllables: ***Hear, Israel, speak****eth* and ***heed****ed*. The G$\#_5$ on the syllable **heed** in particular will require additional modification if its timbre is to match the rest of the phrase.

Verdi is often criticized for increasing the dramatic demands he places on the soprano voice well beyond what his predecessors required. Yet for the most part he merely expands previously realized potentials, particularly in matters of registration. From *La traviata*, the famous first twenty-one measures of Violetta's great recitative "E strano! è strano!," despite an occasional exciting excursion into upper voice, provide ideal middle-voice registration training. They should be repeated as a unit several times in the original tonality, keeping vowel integrity intact while modifying the pitches above F$_5$ so that they are no brighter than those of upper middle voice. Regardless of dramatic agitation and alternation of short and long phrases requiring rapid breath renewal, inhalation ought to remain completely silent.

An equally fine Verdian exercise for middle-register equalization (with temporary climactic excursion into upper range) and for the juxtaposition of front and back vowels comes from the same aria with "dell' universo, dell' universo intero, misterioso, misterioso, altero, croce, croce e delizia, croce e delizia, delizia al cor." Verdi does not abandon bel canto phrase constructions in his quasi-verismo mode.

REGISTRATION IN SOPRANO UPPER VOICE

With regard to vowel integrity and vowel modification in upper range, it has already been noted that the female voice exhibits a number of acoustic factors that are different from those of male voices. Further clarification is in order.

Because the number of prominent harmonic partials becomes reduced as the fundamental is raised, the soprano exhibits roughly only half the number of overtones when singing her high C (C_6) as does the tenor singing his high C (C_5). Although in present-day notation of almost all vocal literature middle-voice A is written as A440 for both tenor and soprano, he is actually singing A220, an octave lower than she. At an octave higher (high A) the soprano is singing 880 Hz, the tenor 440 Hz. The soprano, then, when singing the identically *written* high note, has some excuse for not maintaining as clear vowel integrity as the tenor, because her fundamental has fewer defining harmonics than his. For that reason, vowel definition at high pitch levels will undergo more modification for her than it does for the male.

In both cases, the identity of the migrating vowel is aided by psychoacoustic filtering provided by the listener's ear. In arriving at perception, the linguistically routined listener will supply the lacking identifying features of the vowel so long as harmonic strength in the spectral region of vowel definition is retained. Yet, regardless of the modification process, vowel tracking must remain, or linguistic intelligibility will be lost.

Recognition of differences in acoustic phenomena between genders should not be a pretext for neglecting soprano diction in the upper middle range and from G_5 upward. Vowel distortion at the *secondo passaggio* and above is unnecessary. In the historic international school of professional vocalism, vowel integrity is maintained in the singing voice even above the *secondo passaggio*. It is true that a soprano will become shrill if she sings the vowel [i] with the same phonetic exactitude at $B\flat_5$ as she does an octave lower at $B\flat_4$ (or as she sings it yet another octave lower at $B\flat_3$). She must alter her mouth and jaw postures. However, there is no reason why the vowel [i] in pitches above the soprano's *secondo passaggio* should become a distant vowel as when Italian *vita* becomes *vawtaw*, English *hero* turns into *huhruh*, or French *été* disintegrates into *uhtuh*. Nor should Pamina need substitute *die Labe* for *die Liebe*.

Pamina's *"Ach, ich fühl's"* (*Die Zauberflöte*, Mozart) poses a masterful challenge in soprano registration. Although equally usable as a study for bridging breath energy from lower middle to upper range, the aria makes an excellent upper-voice vowel modification study. A number of its sustained phrases place front vowels at pitches in high range: "es *ist* verschwunden," "hin der *Liebe* Gluck!" and "meinem *Herzen* mehr zurück." It is as though Mozart, using the front vowels [i], [e] and [ɛ] had composed a vocal study in upper-range vowel modification.

By appropriately opening her mouth for rising pitch, Pamina minimizes the acoustic energy that normally increases in lateral vowels that are sung at high pitches. *Aggiustamento* induces a natural process of graduated vowel transformation. There

EXAMPLE 10.11.

EXAMPLE 10.12.

EXAMPLE 10.13.

need be no sudden loss of vowel integrity, no "shifting of gears," no "hooking in" at or above the *passaggio* pivotal point.

A number of the swiftly moving excerpts from the literature presented in chapter 5 for developing agility are equally applicable for developing easy entrance into upper voice. As in all ranges of the voice, it is wisest when working in upper voice to alternate between rapidly moving and slow, sustained passages. A traditional exercise (ex. 10.11) for arriving in upper range by means of sustained vocalization is a slow pattern on the ascending octave arpeggio, followed by descent on the dominant seventh chord. Lateral and rounded vowel series should both be employed through the keys of A, B♭, B, and C.

Similar assistance in upper-range extension is offered by a rapid exercise constructed on the arpeggiated tenth (ex. 10.12). It should first be sung on a single vowel, followed by the alternation of lateral and rounded vowels. In the middle of each phrase, a change from a lateral to a rounded vowel (or from rounded to lateral) may occur on the repeated tenth of the scale.

The arpeggiated pattern of example 10.11 can be favorably extended over a wider range, as in example 10.13. A more advanced maneuver (ex. 10.14) is a slow arpeggiated tenth followed by a descending scale passage. The pattern should be sung sequentially through at least the tonalities of G♭, G, and A♭.

Examples 10.11, 10.12, 10.13, and 10.14 draw attention to proper vowel modification (as opposed to vowel distortion), thereby ensuring register equalization. However, while retaining vowel integrity, some neutralization of vowel definition must ensue in the mounting scale, or the resulting timbre will be shrill.

EXAMPLE 10.14.

EXAMPLE 10.15.

From the literature itself come potential vocalises that serve the advanced singer as vehicles for systematically developing upper-range extension. Although the entire aria may not be a viable part of a singer's performance repertory, melismatic passages from Violetta's "*Sempre libera*" (*La traviata*, Verdi) provide a worthwhile registration study (ex. 10.15). The passage can be executed consecutively, on lateral and rounded vowels, then with the original text. Although the vowel [ɑ] is generally substituted at these moments for the vowel [i] on *follie* and *gioir* (partly as a practical means to avoid the excessive brilliance that the vowel [i] demonstrates at high pitch), there remains the danger of shrillness unless the vowel [ɑ] is modified by some increase in mouth opening above the *secondo passaggio*. (The vowel [i], if retained by the performer, must approach further neutralization at $D\flat_6$–C_6.) This should be accomplished without loss in elevation of the cheek area, at the same time avoiding the exaggerated smile position. Neither foolishly grinning nor dropping the jaw is the answer.

For the technically advanced large lyric or dramatic soprano, a passage (ex. 10.16) from Leonora's "*Tacea la notte*" (*Il trovatore*, Verdi), extending from "al cor, al guardo estatico la terra un ciel sembrò," makes an excellent study in registration and range extension. It can be accomplished on a single vowel, on inherent vowels of the text, or with the original text. As lower middle voice moves into upper range, an even scale is made possible by gradual *aggiustamento*.

In the "*Willow Song*" from *The Ballad of Baby Doe* (Douglas Moore), the passage beginning "Oh willow" and extending through "Pray tell him I am weeping, too"

EXAMPLE 10.16.

bró, la ter-ra un ciel, un ciel sem-bró, al cor,___ al guar - do e - sta - ti - co la

ter - ra un ciel sem - bró, la ter - ra_____un___ciel sem -

EXAMPLE 10.17.

Wil - low, when our love was new,___ Wil - low, if he once should

be re - turn - ing, Pray tell___him I am weep-ing too.___

(ex. 10.17) makes a telling registration and vowel-modification drill for the lyric soprano voice. The approach to D_6 (high D) in upper voice begins in lower middle register. Some sopranos will find this sudden upward leap from a low tessitura advantageous, others may consider it problematic. (An *appoggio* increase should begin just before leaving the low note, not when arriving at the high note.) In practice sessions, lateral and rounded vowels may be substituted for the vowels of the text. Because of its direct application on the middle syllable of *returning*, the mixed vowel [oe] is recommended as a vocalization device for the entire passage. Then the original text of the excerpt ought to be sung with fitting union of vowel definition and *aggiustamento*.

The arias *"Ain't It a Pretty Night?"* and *"The Trees on the Mountain"* (*Susannah*, Floyd) have frequent excursions from lower to upper range, offering numerous phrases that the sizable soprano voice can profitably excerpt for vowel modification and *passaggio* study. (With its sostenuto demands, its range extension, and its full orchestration, the role of Susannah is not an appropriate vehicle for the distinctly lyric voice.)

The best way to ensure vocal freedom throughout the soprano voice is to first establish unrestricted vocalism in the long middle register. Although it is true that soubrettes and light lyrics may have the earliest access to upper range, in the registration training of most sopranos it is inappropriate to expect remarkable upper-range extension before ease of production has been established in the long middle range. After this has been accomplished, exercises that involve the two extremes of the vocal compass should be introduced in equal measure.

Registration timbres are best examined in relation to the technical accomplishment of the individual voice; the exact sequence of registration work will vary with the individual. The large lyric or dramatic soprano voice is just as much in need of flexibility and pyrotechnical skill as is the soubrette/coloratura but may come to it somewhat later.

Exercises dealing with high and low range extensions are of equal importance. At this point in a systematic approach to voice technique, either region could be considered next. Literature passages and exercises that exhibit extreme upper-range extension will be treated first; thereafter, low-range exercises and literature passages dealing with low range will be the object of study.

It is time to look systematically at the development of the stratospheric soprano register.

FLAGEOLET REGISTER

The highest pitch extensions of the female voice are described by a variety of registration terms in several languages: *flageolet, voce di campanello,* and *die zweite Höhe;* in English, flageolet, piccolo, flute, or bell register. The timbre results from the uppermost extension of traditional "head voice" function.

As noted in chapter 3, the process of damping (or dampening) comes prominently into play in the extreme upper range of the female voice: the vocal folds elongate, their mass diminishes, and firm vocal-fold occlusion occurs over the membranous segment, that is, the vibrating portion of the glottis. (The cartilaginous portion of the vocal fold is not involved in phonatory vibration in any range.) Significantly, in the soprano's stratospheric range, only the anterior (forward) portion of the vocal folds is set into vibration. This phenomenon in the female singing voice, the flageolet register, is verifiable through flexible fiberoptic–stroboscopic observation.

Regardless of voice category, every voice is bound by an ultimate pitch at either end of its negotiable scale: each singer has an upper-range limitation dependent on the extent to which vocal-fold elongation can occur, while lower-range limitation is dependent on the degree to which the thyroarytenoids avert potential stretching of the vocal folds.

Flageolet register guarantees the fullest elongation and thinning of the folds in a range of the voice that often remains neglected. Contrariwise, unmodified chest timbre depends on a set of laryngeal conditions in which the thickest and shortest vocal-fold configurations are operative. This full ("pure," "raw," or "open") chest register is frequently not wholly explored. Exercises that develop all registration capabilities allow a soprano to make complete use of her entire range, from the bottom note to the top.

EXAMPLE 10.18.

The flageolet maneuver induces psychological and physical release in the upper extremes of the soprano range. Flageolet requires aesthetic risk-taking and the letting go of all conscious control. Practicing the flageolet brings freedom to the entire upper range and eases the tasks a soprano later encounters in high-lying pitches of the performance literature. Flageolet timbre is best accomplished in an almost childlike manner, executing rapid patterns imitative of hilarious laughter.

Several nonsinging maneuvers are preparatory to the flageolet exercises. Have the soprano imitate light, high, laughter, repeated a number of times. Teacher and student should join together in such hilarity. Equally useful is the imitation of a rapid siren sound, from low to high range, aiming at no specific pitch; at each repetition the glissando motif is tossed higher and higher. A keyboard check of the height of pitches reached by gay laughter and the siren imitation will often surprise the singer. Sometimes it is best to have several sopranos work on flageolet together, each giving the other courage. A singer must be willing to cast aside all reserve and enter into a spirit of utter abandonment.

For some sopranos, singing the fast-moving flageolet vocalises in staccato rather than legato mode is more conducive to freedom. Each singer must experiment as to which mode brings the most favorable results.

A grateful pattern is example 10.18, rhythmically and rapidly executed in shifting tonalities without hesitation between consecutive keys. In early attempts at flageolet, pitch accuracy and vocal quality may not be perfect. Both will improve as courage and skill develop.

Other patterns that mount into the highest regions of the singing voice, based on arpeggios, scale passages, and short agility exercises, should be constructed. Sostenuto exercises ought not to be used for development of the flageolet voice, or at least not in the early stages of its development.

Once she has discovered flageolet function, the soubrette, soubrette/coloratura, or light lyric soprano may well be able to produce pitches through G_6 (a perfect fifth above high C [C_6]). Some light soprano voices can continue upward to B_6 or C_7, a full octave above high C. (In the rarest of cases, C_8 is possible.) Flageolet range is, of course, most extensive in the soubrette/coloratura category of soprano voice. Dramatic soprano voices cannot be expected to carry flageolet to the same heights as do lighter instruments, because the upper *passaggi* points of dramatic voices occur at lower points in the musical scale.

The dramatic soprano should aim at producing flageolet as high as $C\sharp_6$ (or D_6), the *Zwischenfach* soprano (and the mezzo-soprano) to B_5 or C_6. Even the true contralto (an exceedingly rare instrument) ought to attempt to routine flageolet at high-lying pitches comparable for her category (A_5 or $B\flat_5$).

Some successful professional female singers who have difficulty in producing flageolet would find more freedom in upper voice were they able to let go of habitual static controls that inhibit full elongation and damping of the vocal folds. As mentioned above, the vocal folds have a membranous portion that participates in vibratory function and a cartilaginous portion that does not. Although elongation and damping processes of the membranous folds reach their greatest fulfillment in flageolet register, to a lesser degree they are operative in all the highest pitches of a soprano voice. To some extent, then, flageolet is simply a continuance of the approach for all high-lying pitches in the female voice.

A number of pitches possible in flageolet range lodge above those required for public performance. The advantage of developing flageolet capability lies in the ease it brings to the exposed pitches of high-lying literature. Having drilled the flageolet register to $E\flat_6$ or above, high C (C_6) is no longer the top performable note for Mimì. She has assurance that she can produce a number of semitones beyond high C.

After the singing voice has been fully warmed up through breath management, agility, vowel differentiation, resonance balancing, and sostenuto exercises, a few additional minutes spent drilling flageolet register should be part of the daily technical routining for every soprano, regardless of *Fach*. For dramatic sopranos, the suggested patterns may be transposed downward a semitone, a whole tone, or a minor third. For soubrette, coloratura, and lyric instruments, they may be transposed upward a semitone, a whole tone, or a minor third.

Literature segments that act as flageolet vocalises abound. As is often the case when vocal technique is an issue, the most adaptable and productive come from Mozart. A brief *Die Zauberflöte* segment (ex. 10.19) from the Queen of the Night's great pyrotechnical aria makes a perfect introductory literature companion to example 10.18. The pattern should be sung on various vowels. A good maneuver is to begin at a lower key level than the original tonality, then move upward by semitone as far as possible.

For the lyric soprano, a useful figure (ex. 10.20) from "*Caro nome*" begins with "l'ultimo mio sospir" (*Rigoletto*, Verdi) and extends through the intervallic leaps in sixths at *a te*. This exercise has particular merit in that it encompasses a two-octave range. The much-discussed principles of vowel definition and modification are emi-

EXAMPLE 10.19.

EXAMPLE 10.20.

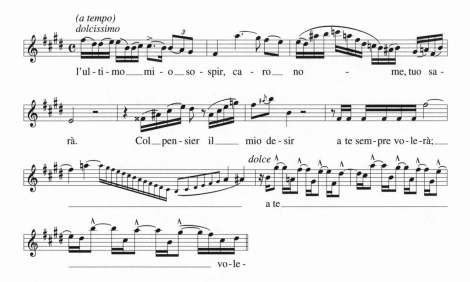

nently required in this passage: speech-inflection postures in lower range (*si canta come si parla*), graduated mouth opening in the middle and upper ranges. (It is traditional to substitute the vowel [ɑ] for the vowel [e] at the *a te* passage.) This vocalise should be passed through several ascending tonalities to induce reliance on the flageolet timbre in the highest notes. Then the passage in its original tonality will become much more secure.

For the soubrette or coloratura, an outstanding flageolet prototype (ex. 10.21) comes from the concluding measures of "*Je suis Titania*" (*Mignon*, Thomas). The repeated octave intervals ascending by semitones require jaw mobility. The leap of a minor tenth (C_5 to $E\flat_6$) requests flexible adjustment of the resonator tract with the mouth

EXAMPLE 10.21.

well open on $E\flat_6$. As has been recommended for previously cited flageolet exercises, portions of this excerpt may be isolated for transposition into neighboring tonalities.

In the *Mignon* excerpt, trills are indicated at F_5, G_5, $G\sharp_5$ and A_5. In this instance, the trill itself happens below the flageolet range. In fact, composers mostly request that trilling take place in upper middle and upper ranges. Trill usually occurs at the interval of a minor or a major second. Its appearance in example 10.21 provides an opportunity to discuss the technique of trilling in general.

Garcia's description of trill remains pertinent:[2] "a rapid, equal, and distinct alternation of two notes at the distance of a major or minor second, according to the position of the trill in the scale."

The only time the larynx should actively oscillate is during the execution of trill. Although both vibrato and trill are pitch variants, vibrato is not induced by a consciously oscillating larynx, whereas trill results from intentional rapid laryngeal oscillation.

As noted elsewhere on the sensation of trilling and its pedagogic value:[3]

> When trilling is first attempted, the oscillatory motion of the larynx may feel
> somewhat wild and uncontrolled. It is exactly therein that its advantage as a
> freedom-inducing device lies. . . . Letting the larynx suddenly engage in such
> loose movement can free the instrument. . . . Because of the size and weight
> of some vocal instruments, and because of corresponding registration events,
> the trill may be more difficult to execute in the robust voice than in the more
> lyric instrument. (The trill of the "nightingale" soprano is far less impressive
> than that of . . . the spinto soprano.)

Ingo Titze, discussing the relationship of trill to vibrato, remarks:[4]

> The basic difference between a vocal trill and vibrato is that the average pitch
> is raised in trill, but not in vibrato. In trill there is a deliberate attempt to

alternate between a base note and a higher note (either a semitone up or a whole tone up), whereas in vibrato the attempt is to remain on the same note. . . . Thus, trill is considerably more demanding on the pitch-changing mechanism than vibrato because a larger F_0 [fundamental frequency] change must be executed in a shorter amount of time.

Even if apocryphal, the story of Cotogni as a boy treble shaking his leg to produce trill illustrates that laryngeal oscillation is essential to trilling. (Shaking the leg [or the head] is not a recommended procedure.) For the adult soprano, a pitch level in upper middle range may be the most rewarding starting point for learning trill.

A somewhat bizarre but often successful device for learning the sung trill is to have the singer trill a sustained whistle on a single pitch, then immediately to sing the same note with similar laryngeal motion and breath management, taking note of the extent of laryngeal oscillation in each maneuver. (This device is also sometimes useful in helping the straight-tone singer to find vibrato.)

The composer of the *Mignon* excerpt of example 10.21 seems to have been fully aware of the desirable location for the onset of soprano trilling. The sixteenth-note embellishment figure following each trill joins a brief agility pattern with trilling, both of which are freedom-inducing maneuvers. The soprano may wish to select out the trill measures of example 10.21 as ideal devices for further detailed study. It is helpful initially to introduce each trill with a small agility figure built on the interval of a second, just as the composer Thomas has done in this instance, or an agility motif that encompasses the interval of a minor or major third. Some singers feel a natural affinity with trill execution, while others require considerable time to achieve it. As with flageolet timbre, trill is a freedom-inducing procedure. Yet a soprano should avoid excessive trilling, or at least be on guard that the increased degree of laryngeal oscillation not persist as an assisted vibrato (motion at the level of the external larynx that is not the result of internal laryngeal neurologic impulses).

It is suitable that this section dealing with access to the stratospheric soprano range conclude with selections from the master composer of soprano vocal literature. For the light lyric soprano voice, Blöndchen's "*Durch Zärtlichkeit*" (*Die Entführung aus dem Serail*, Mozart) is the ultimate study in flexibility and range extension. The mounting scale passages of example 10.22 are unbeatable as transposable figures (depending on the individual instrument, taking them lower and higher) for flageolet study. Mozart's first version of the running scale encompasses a tenth, the second a twelfth; both move from lower middle voice into flageolet areas. En route there will be gradual mouth opening, without loss of the zygomatic lift. An exaggerated smile posture (lateral pulling of the lips) should be avoided on the highest pitches, but a pleasant expression must remain. The repeated notes on high E_6 should have the clear bell-ringing timbre of flageolet without shrillness, to match the rest of the scale.

For the dramatic coloratura, or for the lyric soprano with ease in coloratura extension, passages from Constanze's great aria from the same opera is a classic device

EXAMPLE 10.22.

EXAMPLE 10.23.

for flageolet drill (ex. 10.23). In addition to its flageolet adaptability, this excerpt incorporates reiterated onsetting in upper range and velocity coursing in ascending and descending patterns between low voice and upper voice (and return) that extend from low B_3 through high D_6. As with other vocalization material, this pattern may be transposed to tonalities other than the original, either above it or below.

Finally, for coloraturas, much of the Queen of the Night aria, from which the brief passage of example 10.19 was earlier excerpted, represents the upper-range extension exercise par excellence. Phrases from these Mozartean quotations, in transposition as well as in the original tonalities, should be broken down into sequential patterns for frequent repetition, then reassembled.

With soprano voices of light construction and timbre, it is essential that, in the uppermost range, flageolet technique be incorporated directly into public performance. Even the dramatic coloratura will need some publicly performable pitches produced in flageolet timbre. In spite of their individual differences in vocal weight, singers of the Queen of the Night, Blöndchen, Constanze, Violetta, and even the *Il trovatore* Leonora will profit by extending the upper range through daily flageolet practice.

MIXTURES AND CHEST

It would be a mistake to assume that technical work on low-voice mixtures and chest-voice timbres should be delayed until all other ranges have been firmly established. In exploring voice registration in a systematic way, each of the registers needs separate attention (but not intentional separation), with the final aim of a seamless scale. The long middle register is the obvious beginning point. As soon as technical progress in middle voice has been made, a female may confidently turn to work on the equalization of register transitions from upper middle to upper voice and from lower middle to low voice. The low range of the voice is here considered last simply in the interest of orderly presentation.

Most sopranos center their speech-inflection range around the B_3–$E^\flat_4$ region of the scale, reserving the pitches of upper middle voice ($C^\sharp_5$–$F^\sharp_5$) for laughter and for emotionally heightened, excited speech. They tend to avoid pitches of the lower middle register that extend upward from E_4 through C_5; this lower middle portion of the voice often experiences limited use in daily life. Therefore, a number of sopranos detect a weakness around C_5 or B_4 that may extend downward to $E^\flat_4$ (the Melba point). A single pitch, or several pitches, may give the feeling that there is a "hole" at that point in the vocal scale. This "hole" is because of an imbalance between infrequently used registration mixtures.

Historic pedagogy suggests "bringing down head voice" into the lower middle region. This means restricting the vibratory function of the vocal folds to the vocal ligament, thereby reducing or avoiding excursion into the vocalis muscle. When overreliance on chest timbres has been habitual, "bringing head" downward is a good method for improving timbre in the lower middle region. However, in pursuing this generally commendable goal, there is a danger of limiting activity almost entirely to the inner portion of the vocal folds. Too much head function in this lower middle range will inhibit intensity and produce limited depth in the quality of the middle-to-low transitional area, contributing to a "hole" or "holes".

It is not unusual for a sizable soprano, even when she normally speaks at low pitch (vocalis dominant), to produce only thin quality (ligament vibration) when she *sings* in lower middle voice, because she has been taught that she must remain entirely in head on all pitches that do not call for actual chest quality. (The complete avoidance of chest is advocated in some Germanic techniques, because in that culture female chest or chest mixtures are often considered to be unwomanly. By contrast, the traditional Italian school cherishes the sensuality of female chest voice.) Most teachers wisely guard against permitting excessive chest timbre in the emerging soprano voice. But eliminating all mixture in lower middle voice produces timbre lacking in

EXAMPLE 10.24.

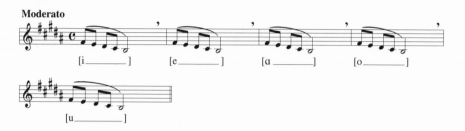

Moderato

[i_____]   [e_____]   [a_____]   [o_____]

[u_____]

depth at the very part of the scale where richness is most needed. In the singing voices of both young and mature sopranos, when there is a noticeable lack of intensity in pitches of low register, corrective registration devices can be applied. A sequence of single vowels should be sung on a single-note pattern, awareness being directed to the kinds of mixture and open chest timbres that are possible on an identical pitch.

In general, it is easiest to maintain head timbre in low voice on the lateral (front) vowel [i], whereas a rounded (back) vowel such as [ɔ] tends to lend itself more readily to mixture or chest. Degrees of mixture are determined by the extent to which the vocalis muscle is involved.

There can be no isolated control of these laryngeal events; they are *induced by tonal concepts*. The musicianly ear demands the timbre, and the body responds.

The exercises that follow should not be introduced all at once. At first, it is best to spend only a few minutes, late in the practice session, on exercises that develop chest and mixtures in female lower voice. As soon as basic technique has been established, in the practice session low-voice exercises should be alternated with those of other registers.

Patterns that drill the register timbres a soprano can produce in lower middle and low ranges pivot around the Melba point ($E^\flat_4$). A series of descending 5–4–3–2–1 phrases beginning at $F^\sharp_4$ in the key of B is recommended (ex. 10.24). Each of the cardinal vowels [i], [e], [a], [o] and [u] should be employed.

The soprano proceeds with the pattern as follows:

1. begin and remain in head;
2. begin in head, then midway (D_4) introduce head-chest mixtures;
3. begin in head, then midway (D_4) substitute chest-head for head-chest mixtures (D_4);
4. begin in head, then midway (D_4) move directly into chest; and
5. sing the pattern once more entirely in head.

As the pattern moves to lower tonalities, the point at which the timbres alter will change. The purpose of example 10.25 is not to establish an absolute pitch at which

EXAMPLE 10.25.

EXAMPLE 10.26.

timbre is altered; it is to develop the use of all four register functions (head, head-chest, chest-head, and chest) below the Melba point. In addition, each performer, depending on voice category and size, will make her own determination as to where during performance such mixture and chest timbres properly occur in any particular passage.

For the dramatic soprano and the mezzo-soprano these events can be located a semitone or a whole tone above the $E^\flat_4$ pivotal point; they may be initiated even higher in the scale (by another semitone or two) for the true contralto.

If the beginning soprano insists she has no chest-voice function, request her to imitate a few aggressive expressions of low male speech: "No!" "Yes!" "Quiet!" Then making use of a swiftly moving brief pattern, she should imitatively transfer that same "masculine" timbre to the lowest pitches of her singing voice (ex. 10.26). A singer may at first find the results raucous or crude; she may initially resist what to her are offensive open chest sounds. With time she will learn to modify these pitches through mixed timbres and to produce them with pleasure.

An exercise constructed on a slowly ascending arpeggio is the next logical maneuver (ex. 10.27). Pitches below $E^\flat_4$ ($D^\sharp_4$) are first sung in either mixture or chest, those above in head. In the first measure of example 10.27, a dramatic voice may wish to sing the triplet figure entirely in chest, with only A_4 in head. She may even, as an occasional feat, sing the whole figure of measure 1 in chest mixture. The third figure (measure 3) may begin in chest and move to chest-head timbre at $D^\sharp_4$, to head-chest at $F^\sharp_4$, and to head at B_4. A lyric voice will adhere to the Melba point doctrine by not carrying chest upward beyond $E^\flat_4$.

EXAMPLE 10.27.

EXAMPLE 10.28.

EXAMPLE 10.29.

Soon thereafter, a slow arpeggio extending from an upper octave in head to a lower octave in chest is introduced (ex. 10.28). The same process regarding mixtures of head and chest advocated for use in example 10.27 pertains in example 10.28.

Next, a passing tone is inserted into the 8–5–3–1 pattern, between scale degrees 3 and 1. This passing tone on the second note of the scale will be sometimes produced in mixture, sometimes in chest. The aim of the exercise is to change timbres intentionally at varying points in the descending scale. For example, in measure 2 of example 10.29, $D^{\sharp}_4$ may be sung one time in head, one time in mixture, and still another in chest. Then the singer returns to head timbre for execution of the complete measure.

Soprano literature contains many examples of descent from middle to low voice with immediate return to middle voice (from head to chest or mixture, then back to head). Example 10.30 is designed to meet such registration exigencies. The exact degrees of mixed register timbres and of open chest on the lower pitches will depend on the category of soprano. Over the course of many repetitions, a singer should practice all possible mixtures on pitches that occur below $F^{\sharp}_4$ but remain in head for the upper notes.

"*Deh vieni, non tardar*" (*Le nozze di Figaro*, Mozart) provides a fertile source for negotiating a register descent to C_4: "che col dolce sussurro il cor ristaura." The final syllable of *ristaura* should be sung in chest or in some form of chest mixture. If she is to have sufficient intensity and vocal coloration, even the light soprano must make use of chest mixture in a phrase that concludes, as does this one, in low range.

The next two phrases ("qui ridono i fioretti e l'erba è fresca" and "ai piaceri d'amor qui tutto adesca") use intervals that contrast register colors (leap from C_4 [chest] to

EXAMPLE 10.30.

$B\flat_4$ [head] at *qui ridono*, and again, the downward leap from D_5 [head] *d'a-* to C_4 on *-mor* [chest]). From the same source, a phrase such as "tra queste piante ascose!" which descends to C_4 (middle C) on the final syllable, ought to conclude in chest mixture. This latter phrase should be treated as follows:

1. C_4 is first sung entirely in head,
2. then in head-chest mixture,
3. followed by chest-head mixture,
4. next in open chest, and finally,
5. in the most aesthetically pleasing mixture of head and chest, or entirely in chest.

The effect of the succeeding onset an octave above (C_5) on *vieni* will be much enhanced by the juxtaposition of low- and middle-register colors. If the soprano remains entirely in head timbre for these phrases that cross registers the emotional content of both text and music will be lost.

From Gluck's "*O del mio dolce ardor*" comes the exemplary classic phrase "Ovunque il guardo io giro," which descends from middle to low register. Only the soubrette or light lyric will successfully remain entirely in head during its execution, and even with those categories, at least some mixture would be welcome on *giro*.

An outstanding example of the use of registers for emotive purposes is Schumann's "*Heiss mich nicht reden.*" Schumann expresses heartfelt response to the inner meaning of Goethe's poem through vocalism that uses a full palette of female registration colors. Almost every line of this lied could serve as a technical registration exercise. Phrases lie chiefly in the long middle voice—$E\flat_4$ to G_5—yet tessitura is equally balanced between lower middle and upper middle ranges. Varying shades of registration should be examined before determining which brings the most telling response for the individual performer.

Schumann's "Nur ein Gott," at $D\flat_4$–C_4–B_3 (ex. 10.31), must be delivered with as much chest coloration as the singer is capable of giving. The final "Heiss mich nicht reden, heiss mich schweigen" requires play upon mixed and chest timbres. On the octave leap C_4–C_5, the C_4 needs to be as fully in chest as can be managed; the C_5, although in head, ought to retain some of the depth and color of C_4. The final phrase,

Example 10.31.

nur ein Gott! Heiß mich nicht re - den, heiß mich schwei - gen, ein

Schwur drückt mir die Lip-pen zu, und nur ein Gott ver-mag sie auf-zu - schlie-ßen!

Example 10.32.

Nicht ein Lüft - chen regt-sich lei - se, sanft entschlum-mert ruht der

Hain; durch der Blät-ter dun-kle Hül - le stiehlt___ sich lich-ter Son - nen -

schein. Ru - he, ru - he, mei-ne

"und nur ein Gott vermag sie aufzuschliessen!," should never be just "heady"; it should retain mixed-register character. If the soprano has a relatively large instrument, the syllables *Gott* and *schlie* may best be delivered in full chest.

"*Ruhe, meine Seele!*" (Strauss) is a particularly useful study in lower-range registration (ex. 10.32). Despite the soft dynamic, it would be a mistake to sing the opening phrase without attention to crossings among chest, chest mixtures, and head. For example, the G_4–C_4 interval of the fifth on *Ruhe* should augment contrasts between head and chest colors. Throughout the song the singer should try several voice qualities before settling for any one of them; the deep emotion of the lied will thereby be greatly enhanced.

Debussy has been criticized for not making full use of the potentials of the singing instrument, a questionable charge when one considers the sweep of his *Ariettes oubliées*. His handling of registration is traditional in "*C'est l'extase langoureuse*." The

Example 10.33.

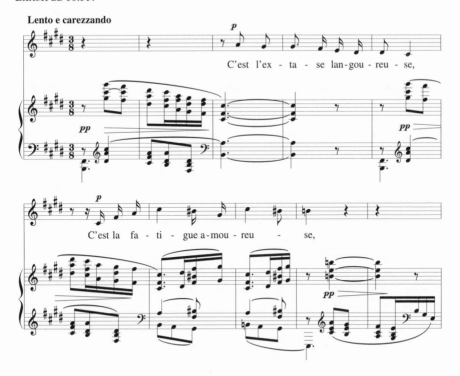

composer plays masterfully on descent from lower middle to low voice (ex. 10.33). The soprano who makes no use of head-chest mixture on the low notes of the descending and ascending phrases may well miss the composer's intent, expressed by the harmonic progressions in the keyboard. The opening vocal phrase, "C'est l'extase langoureuse," should first be practiced entirely in head, then restated with the D_4 and $C\#_4$ of the syllables -*gou-reu-se* in head-chest mixture. The phrase is repeated with the indicated syllables on D_4 and $C\#_4$ executed in chest-head mixture. In a subsequent step, mixtures are retained on D_4, but the final $C\#$ of the phrase (the syllable -*se*) is sung in full chest. Recommencing the phrase, the singer determines which colors produce for her the most convincing interpretation.

Further evidence of Debussy's cognizance of the relationship of both registration and keyboard coloration to dramatic content is illustrated in the same mélodie. The phrase "le roulis sourd des cailloux" should be sung first entirely in head. Then the $D\#_4$, D_4, and $C\#$ can be sung in either head-chest or chest-head mixture. The singer determines which of these colors produces the best aesthetic result and the most physical comfort. Large voices may want to sing the D_4 and the $C\#_4$ of the first syllable of *cailloux* in chest, returning to head on the final syllable ($F\#_4$) of *cailloux*.

Example 10.34.

Continuing with this magnificent mélodie, a full range of hues that play back and forth over registers may be explored. The song serves as a comprehensive vehicle for achieving a unified vocal scale during cross-registration events.

The tessitura of "*Un bel dì vedremo*" (*Madama Butterfly*, Puccini) lies initially in the upper-middle *zona di passaggio*. However, as Butterfly moves into lower middle voice with the phrase "E poi la nave appare," she needs to sing $D^\flat_4$ and $E^\flat_4$ (and possibly F_4 as well) in forms of mixture before again ascending. When Cio-Cio-San is sung by a *lirico spinto* (as she is intended to be—not by a lightweight lyric or coloratura soprano who may match a geisha's physical attributes but not Butterfly's vocal *Fach*), she will retain intensity and mixed timbre in low-lying phrases. If Cio-Cio-San is inappropriately assigned to a light soprano, that singer must, for emotive purposes, introduce a greater degree of mixture in the low passages than she might normally use in the same range when singing some other literatures.

Frau Fluth (*Die lustigen Weiber von Windsor*, Nicolai), in her playful imaginings about the deception she intends to use on Sir John, must describe her hoax in the "ach, ach, ich liebe, liebe Euch" passages by varying her registration hues. The word *Euch* in its first appearance (G_4) will be in head, its next appearance (D_4) in some form of mixture, and its final version ($E^\flat_4$) in chest.

A productive cross-registration workout (ex. 10.34) is intended for the technically secure soprano. It should be sung in only a few tonalities. Once again, during descending passages various registers ought to be introduced.

It is appropriate to conclude this section of registration vocalization material by turning again to Mozart. The role of Fiordiligi (*Così fan tutte*, Mozart) requires a large lyric soprano instrument of dramatic capabilities with an aptitude for sustaining and moving the voice. An excellent study for incorporating chest voice into low-lying pitches in phrases that involve several registers comes from the aria "*Come scoglio*." The passage "contra i venti e la tempesta, e la tempesta" offers registration challenges for even the most well-schooled soprano.

There is no doubt that the first "e la tempesta" $B^\flat_3$–$A^\flat_3$ must be in chest (full chest, if possible). The telling question is what to do on D_4 and $E^\flat_4$ with -*tra i* and *vent*-. It is clear that for emotional and dramatic reasons Mozart wants to point up timbre changes that are the consequence of dropping from the region of the *secondo passaggio* at F_5 to the *primo passaggio* at D_4–$E^\flat_4$, then rocketing upward through middle range to the upper-range $B^\flat_5$ (high B♭). Should D_4 and $E^\flat_4$ be in head, head-chest mixture, chest-head mixture, or full chest? Each soprano must determine which timbre will work best for her, but she can decide only if she has experienced them all. Her answer will depend on the size of her instrument and on her registration facility. In order to make a final decision, she should routine all degrees of mixture and full chest on these notes.

Also from Fiordiligi's great aria comes a passage for cross-registration leaping: "la morte sola," concluding with "far che cangi affetto il cor, far che cangi." For many sopranos the E_4 natural on *sola* is the bête noire: head? mixture? chest? Large lyric and dramatic soprano voices will use a mixture or full chest at this point. Unless a lighter lyric (who may not be cast to best advantage) possesses a very strong lower-range head capability, she will probably prefer to apply a head-chest mixture.

The next decision to be made is how best to handle D_4 at the leap of the tenth from F_5 to D_4 (*che can-*) and the octave leap back from D_4 to D_5 (*-gi af-fet-*). A splendid effect in registration play is achieved if the singer takes D_4 on *can-* with strong chest-register elements. This quality should foretell the color of subsequent timbre that must be full chested on the $B^\flat_3$ of *affetto*, following which there is a return to head on the octave leap to $B^\flat_4$.

Without doubt, the final syllable of the last *cangi* must be sung in a strong full-chest timbre. Although the purist will object, it is traditional (and vocally and dramatically exciting) to move the written fermata from D_5 to low $B^\flat_3$. The situation is bizarre; Fiordiligi's determination should echo it vocally.

Another example from Fiordiligi's pyrotechnical aria serves as important cross-registration material. The scale passage "non vi renda audaci ancor" descends to low A_3 on *-da-* (full chest). It gradually returns to lower middle voice, followed by registration contrasts in the subsequent setting of the same text. The segment provides a complete study in lower registration timbres. All pitches below F_4 should be practiced by the mature lyric or lirico spinto in every combination of chest and chest mixture. For dramatic voices, too, F_4 should be included in this ultimate "register-cise." In drilling it, sometimes only the G_5 will be exempt from either mixture or full chest. In all probability, when returning to a timbre suitable for public performance, the larger soprano instrument naturally tends to use chest mixture in the D_4–F_4 tessitura and full chest on the $B^\flat_3$ and the C_4. For reasons of vocal health, the G_5 and the $B^\flat_5$ must remain entirely in head.

In general, with regard to registration practices in the literature, the closer a soprano instrument tends toward one of the lighter categories, the less use is made of chest and chest mixtures. When the drama calls for it, a sumptuous voice may sing full chest on $E^\flat_4$. The soubrette and the light lyric must never take unmitigated chest timbre up that far in public performance. However, as a practice device, an occasional touching of the $E^\flat_4$ in chest timbre will prove beneficial for almost all soprano voices.

11

Accomplishing Dynamic Control

IT IS DESTRUCTIVE FOR MOST YOUNG SOPRANOS DURING EARLY TRAIN-
ing to attempt the full range of dynamic subtlety that an accomplished artist has
learned to deliver. Much of the coaching of student and preprofessional singers is
less than successful because of rigid adherence to the principle that every voice must
meet the demands for dynamic finesse the composer rightly expects from the fin-
ished artist.

It is unrealistic to require the young soprano to sing at pianissimo or fortissimo
levels in all regions of her voice while she is still in the process of developing basic
technique. Unfortunately, dynamic levels in the singing voice can be altered through
reliance on two faulty devices: (1) admixture of breath in order to reduce decibels,
and (2) pressed glottal closure in order to increase decibels. Less-than-skillful singers,
when attempting to sing piano or pianissimo, are tempted to resort to high airflow
levels, with slack glottal closure, and to produce forte or fortissimo through forced
inward contraction of the breath-management musculature. They press the glottis
tightly to gain greater vocal-fold closure. In so doing they squeeze the laryngeal
sphincter (the glottis), under the erroneous assumption that they are providing
"support." They radically alter their singing technique in order to accomplish the
dynamic changes from piano to forte.

As has been asserted throughout, especially in the discussion regarding breath
management in chapter 4, successful singing is based on a synergy of airflow and
vocal-fold response. A stable foundation for tonal beauty cannot be achieved through
breathy or pressed phonation. How to energize the singing voice while remaining
free remains the chief pedagogic concern for all categories of voice, including both
light and dramatic soprano voices.

Pupils of Giovanni Battista Lamperti reported that the renowned maestro maintained that singing piano is in all respects the same as singing forte, except that it is
softer. One does not mix breath with tone in order to reduce dynamic levels, nor
does one push and squeeze in order to increase dynamic levels. It is essential to first

establish freedom in the singing voice at a moderate dynamic level midway between pianissimo and fortissimo.

The Lamperti doctrine is at odds with techniques that recommend loud calling as an appropriate model for soprano vocal production. It is equally opposed to those who believe a voice should be built on sighing and whispering. Air passing loosely over a slack glottis (as in sighing or whispering) will augment the open phase of each vibratory cycle, whereas tightly occluded vocal folds (as in yelling) will augment the closure phase. Glottal efficiency can be achieved only when the vocal folds offer sufficient but not excessive resistance to airflow. That is why this book began with onset precision.

After the soprano has established good onset, consistency of vibrato, clean vowel definition, and the ability to move and to sustain the voice, and has stabilized the resonance balance throughout most of her vocal range, the time has come to undertake effective exercises in dynamic control. Of course, this is not to assume that up to this point only a single dynamic level pertained throughout vocal instruction. The intention here is that the extremes of dynamic adjustment should be delayed until basic vocal technique has been established. In general, the lighter soprano instrument will be able to begin intensive study of dynamic control sooner than the heavier instrument, because larger voices generally take a longer period of time to reach maturity and to acquire technical stability.

As soon as a singer begins to sing expressively in terms of phrase direction and phrase shaping, word accentuation, and interpretative nuance, dynamic variation becomes a priority. Where to begin the technical work of dynamic control? An established procedure for defining dynamic refinement lies in the *messa di voce*. This device trains the singer to begin at a piano or pianissimo level, crescendo to a forte or fortissimo level, and then return to pianissimo without detriment to the vocal timbre. As indicated previously, in the historic international vocal school it is not appropriate to begin any phonation with breathy sound to "drive in the wedge" of resonant tone in order to produce a higher dynamic level, then subsequently to reintroduce breath for return to a lower dynamic level. The soprano should commence each *messa di voce* task in *voce completa*, that is, with a voice complete in its formants and in its chiaroscuro timbre, maintaining uniform vocal quality at all dynamic levels from pianissimo to fortissimo.

This centuries-old approach begins on one pitch with a single vowel (ex. 11.1). A soprano who has developed professional singing skills should spend several minutes at the close of her daily regimen practicing the *messa di voce* exercises in a limited number of ascending tonalities. It is an advanced exercise that demonstrates the ultimate in technical accomplishment.

With the passage of time, the *messa di voce* can be taken through the *zona di passaggio*, but only the technically well-formed singer should attempt to do so. Perhaps the most developed skill in all of the vocal art is the ability to accomplish the *messa*

EXAMPLE 11.1.

EXAMPLE 11.2.

di voce on every performable note. This accomplishment often remains an ideal, not a reality, even for fine singers.

It may be more practical for the young soprano to divide the exercise into two parts, crescendo and decrescendo, with a breath renewal between the two sections (ex. 11.2). After she has reached a comfortable level of accomplishment on the two-part vocalise, she can return to example 11.1.

Of equal importance is the ability to sing a series of vowels in crescendo and decrescendo while maintaining the phonetic integrity of each vowel. The same single-note pattern may be expanded both as the interrupted *messa di voce* and as the full *messa di voce* exercise (ex. 11.3 and 11.4). The next logical step is to apply the *messa di voce* to changing pitch, as in example 11.5. Both pitch and vowel changes are united in a *messa di voce* pattern (ex. 11.6). Prefacing consonants are then introduced, as in example 11.7.

Once again, it is to the performance literature that the soprano can turn for fuller development of dynamic control, selecting passages that serve as useful vocalization material.

The first such example (ex. 11.8) comes from Giulietta's opening recitative, "Eccomi" (see also ex. 4.14), from "*O quante volte!*" (*I Capuleti e i Montecchi*, Bellini). It lies in middle voice and is typical of stylistic considerations that demand a *messa di voce*, even when there is no written indication. The first syllable of the word "*Ecco*" must be sustained by beginning at pianissimo level, followed by a crescendo to forte, then with a return to pianissimo. In this instance, the effect of elongation of a short spoken syllable to accommodate the *messa di voce* in the singing voice is remarkably expressive. Of course, because in spoken Italian the syllable "*Ecc-*" with its doubled [k] phoneme would be a short vowel, following the interpolated *messa di voce* the soprano must take great care to make an exaggerated full stop (silence) for the [k] phoneme. This brief passage should first be drilled in neighboring keys, then, as skill develops, sung at new key levels well into upper voice.

The opening phrase of Handel's "*Alma mia*" is another example of a typical stylistic use of *messa di voce*. Appropriate for all sopranos who wish to improve *messa*

EXAMPLE 11.3.

[i - e - a - o - u]   [u - o - a - e - i]

EXAMPLE 11.4.

[i - e - a - o - u - o - i - e - a]

EXAMPLE 11.5.

EXAMPLE 11.6.

a. [e - ɔ e - ɔ ɔ - e, ɔ - e, ɔ]
b. [ɔ - e. ɔ - e. e - ɔ, e - ɔ, e]

EXAMPLE 11.7.

a. [ve - va, ve - va - ve]
b. [va - ve, va - va]

EXAMPLE 11.8.

Ec - co - mi in lie - ta ve - sta... Ec - comi a - dor - na... come vit - ti - ma all'a - ra.

di voce capabilities, it is especially gratifying for young singers. For systematic technical study, chromatic key progressions are recommended.

The phrase "d'aller là-bas vivre ensemble," from Duparc's "*L'invitation au voyage*" (previously cited in chapter 7 with regard to French nasal vowels), offers an excellent *messa di voce* exercise for the large lyric or dramatic soprano instrument. The phrase should be repeated rhythmically in several keys, then transposed upward and downward into neighboring tonalities, making certain that timbre remains intact during dynamic shading.

Samuel Barber indicates a number of *messa di voce* passages in his invaluable song literature. "*St. Ita's Vision*" (*Hermit Songs*) has three neighboring phrases that are shaped through means of the composer's *messa di voce* indications: "Save, o tiny nursling you. . . . By my heart ev'ry night, You I nurse are not a churl, but were begot on Mary the Jewess by Heaven's light." Similarly, the opening phrase of "*Rain Has Fallen*" (op. 10, no. 1) follows the same dynamic indication, as does the long phrase "Staying a little by the way of mem'ries shall we depart." The rest of the song takes on a *messa di voce* shape spread out over several impassioned phrases which are heightened by a climactic pianoforte interjection. These several passages will prove useful to sopranos of all categories and are ideal for excerption as vocalizing material.

For the advanced soprano of established skill (but not for the soubrette or light lyric), Susannah's "*Ain't it a Pretty Night?*" (*Susannah*, Floyd) offers challenging, rangy phrases built on dynamic variation.

Each soprano should search through her performance literature to find *messa di voce* passages that lie well in her instrument. She can alternate several such passages with the systematized *messa di voce* vocalises suggested above. Mastering *messa di voce* technique prepares the singer for any potential phrase shaping with regard to changing intensity. Some phrases mount from piano to forte, others from forte to piano. In much of the operatic literature, ascending pitch and increased decibels go together, whereas in much of the song literature the reverse is not uncommon, especially in the mélodie. Selections from the literature can be chosen as samples for drilling both phenomena.

12

The Daily Regimen

In PREVIOUS CHAPTERS, SPECIFIC AREAS OF VOCAL TECHNIQUE WERE identified, and exercises were devised for improvement of vocal skills. Regardless of the category of soprano, the entire instrument should be daily exercised in a systematic way.

It is doubtful that even an established singer who performs a wide range of literature will, on a daily basis, cover most areas of technical skill. If she is performing the Schumann *Frauenliebe und -leben*, the Mahler *Rückert Lieder*, or the Debussy *Chansons de Bilitis*, the singer will not be using much of her upper range. Conversely, if she is singing high-lying melismatic material such as the Bach *Jauchzet Gott* or sustained literature with a high tessitura such as the Mozart "*L'amerò*," she will be temporarily restricting her vocalization to specialized range demands. Yet for the sake of healthy vocalism, a brief but thorough daily regimen must cover all aspects of technique.

From specific areas that include onset, breath management, agility, vowel definition, consonant articulation, sostenuto, voice registration and vowel modification, resonance balancing, range extension, and dynamic control, each singer should select a representative series of vocalises, constituting about a thirty-minute routine (to include appropriate pauses, and short rests between the more strenuous exercises). Vocalises ought to move progressively from those of brief onset to those of extensive range-development tasks at both extremes of the scale, and they ought eventually to cover the gamut of dynamic variation. This routine properly marks the beginning of all daily vocal activity. Later in the day, specific areas of technique are singled out for additional work, and complete songs and arias, a role, or a recital program is sung. A singer must not immediately dive into strenuous singing without having first sung through the daily regimen.

For an established artist, it is wise to limit actual singing to no more than an hour and a half per day, and not all at one session. Younger singers must be careful not to overwork the instrument before a firm technical foundation has been built.

In addition to the health benefits that derive from such a daily habit, the singer will know where she stands with regard to the condition of her instrument. For many reasons—physical, environmental, and psychological—a singer is not always in the same vocal shape, sometimes feeling in voice while at other times out of voice, without always being able to identify an exact cause. The daily regimen reveals whether additional warm-up is essential, or if restraint should be exercised.

It is a mistake to wait until shortly before performance time to try out the voice. On a performance day, the wise singer will be up at a reasonable hour, will breakfast (part of the warm-up process), and shortly thereafter will sing through the daily regimen. Then she ought to stay mostly quiet for the remainder of the day, resting and avoiding unnecessary talk and strenuous activity. Shortly before the performance itself, she should spend no more than a few minutes in singing brief rapid vocalises that encompass the entire range. Before publicly performing, she ought to avoid sustained singing, and above all, she should not "pass" parts of the recital or the role with her accompanist in order to assure herself that her voice and her memory are working well. Some performers sing the bloom off the voice in a too-vigorous warm-up session prior to going on stage. No matter how sturdy the vocal technique, it is not wise to sing the role or the concert twice in the same evening; the onstage second performance will lack freshness. A well-schooled singer does not have to prove to herself that she can make it through the programmed material, having routined it in advance with great frequency.

In general, the soubrette warms up more quickly than does the dramatic soprano. The larger the instrument, the more time it may require to become pliable. A Marschallin who warms up onstage during her first entrance frequently remains out of voice for half the act, and she tires more quickly.

Most sopranos notice that with maturity the warm-up time can be conveniently reduced (but not the daily regimen). With an aging singer, however, the warm-up may need to be extended over a longer period of time, with more extensive pauses between maneuvers.

The singer who, on a daily basis, is willing to systematically employ all aspects of the technical reservoir will reap rewards in vocal prowess and performance security. Unless the technical problems of the singing instrument are solved, a singer cannot be an expressive artist, successfully responding with beauty of vocal tone to text, drama, and music. The ultimate goal of performance preparation—artistic communication—is possible only when vocal freedom has been established. Such freedom is the result of the daily technical discipline.

13

The Wedding of Emotion and Skill

Can Violetta manage technical control of her breath and accomplish the pyrotechnical aspects of her first-act aria while experiencing the high levels of emotion she is expected to convey? Can Butterfly undergo such an emotional crisis that she might be tempted to thrust the ceremonial sword into her torso, while at the same time producing appropriate registration modification and resonance balancing in high tessitura? Can Gilda ecstatically recall her lover while skillfully managing her melismas? What is the relationship between dramatic situation and technical prowess, between communication and physical control? How does one keep the text and the drama from robbing one of one's voice?

If, in her mounting emotion, Andromache were to personally experience the excruciating pain involved in the decision to throw her beloved child over the cliff, she would be in no condition to phonate stunning vocal timbre over long sustained phrases leading to a fermata on $B^\flat_5$. Were Salome's perverted sensuality actual, her infatuation with the severed head of John the Baptist would distract her from managing the Straussian vocal line. Along with Violetta, Cio-Cio-San, and Gilda, Andromache and Salome must be able to simultaneously sing and portray the drama because they know technically how to simulate intense passion without actually experiencing it fully. These protagonists are experiencing the action of the role, not the actual deed. While believing in the emotions of the character in which she has been cast, the singer remains the vehicle for its expression, not its personal embodiment.

Does this mean that singers who represent these diverse characters are imparting to their audiences emotions they themselves are not fully experiencing? Of course! No one in the theater, be it the opera stage or legitimate drama, is personally experiencing in full the emotions involved in the roles being enacted. Art is not reality. Art is the ability to portray reality through the comprehension (not the experiencing) of all the emotions that any person may be forced to encounter. To acquire the ability to simulate the entire gamut of human emotions, which far exceeds what any individual can ever expect to personally encounter, is to successfully ply one's craft to its fullest artistic realization.

Problems may develop for a singer if in the hope of achieving believable communication of the drama she is urged by the stage director or coach to submerge herself completely in the emotion of the text. As a result, we find her weeping through, rather than singing, Mimì's final scene, or grieving vocally in *Frauenliebe und -leben*. Analogously, in *Dichterliebe* we sometimes hear male vocal disintegration, not textual enhancement; and the Rodolfo who became so emotionally involved that he was unable to sing the final "Mimì! Mimì!" failed himself, the composer, and the drama. Such inadequacies result from mistaken concepts regarding truth in artistic communication.

With respect to performance communication, the ultimate question comes down to how one unites technical skill with artistic expression. The more efficient the technical skill, the greater the potential for artistic expression. Skill in singing is not the product of raw emotion. Skill results from the programming of physical, acoustic, and controlled emotional responses into one gestalt. Technique and communication comprise the psychology of artistic performance. They are fused into one action. How is the acquisition of dependable skill and its use as a vehicle for communication accomplished?

The sequential development of artistic singing parallels that of artistic figure-skating, artistic dancing, and artistic tennis playing. The professional skater, the ballet dancer, and the tennis champion do not reach their goals by first assuming the emotional stance of an artist, but by learning the tools of the trade that free them for artistic activity. One learns how to execute the triple axel (in some cases even the quadruple axel!), how to leap into the air and turn, how to return the serve over the net, and how to sing the $D^\flat_6$ with graceful ease not by engaging publicly in spur-of-the-moment emotional bathing but by having previously disciplined the body and the mind to those accomplishments. Then the surge of excitement, the flow of adrenaline, and the powers of animal grace are free to come into play.

Great singing is not restricted to artists of the past. Outstanding artists exist today. There are also a number of current fine artists who have remaining technical faults which they at times are able to overcome in performance and at times not. The problem for today's insecure performing artist is partly the proliferation of information. The ambient instructional air that today's singer breathes is full of pedagogic pollutants, often based either on imagery that has no link to acoustic or physical function, or on pseudoscientific assumptions that have no relationship to professional vocal sound. Whereas universalism of vocal timbre would seem to have been the performance model of the nineteenth century and of the first half of the twentieth century, today there are numerous idiosyncratic tonal concepts based on parochial systems that stem from national, regional, or pseudoscientific sources. "New" techniques of singing and "new" pedagogies periodically emerge.

When voice "science" began to surface in the 1940s and the early 1950s, most singers and teachers of singing tended to disregard it as having little practical application to performance. After all, the argument ran, over several centuries professional singers had sung very well without much knowledge regarding physiology and acoustics.

However, the history of vocal pedagogy attests that great teachers of the past were intensely interested in voice function, making use of all the then-available acoustic and physiologic information. (It was a voice teacher, not a scientist or physician, who in the mid-nineteenth century invented the laryngoscope and who was the first person to observe vocal-fold action during phonation.) Visual and audio feedback have always been part of the voice teacher's pedagogic arsenal. One does not use the means of modern analytic instrumentation to invent new techniques of singing but to authenticate degrees of efficiency among various pedagogic measures from both past and present. Voice technique that depends largely on personal charisma, on a collection of unrelated experimental devices, on trial and error, or on collages of wily personal stratagems cannot produce healthy, reliable vocalism. That which is most efficient in phonetic production is aesthetically most pleasing to the knowledgeable listener. Specificity of pedagogic language is essential.

If during performance the soprano artist is occupied with trying to control sound, "placing" the voice in various locations, "opening" her throat, "enlarging" her pharynx, "elevating" her soft palate, engaging sphincters, pushing outward or pulling inward on muscle groups of the torso, there is little chance for a successful wedding of art and technique.

The artistic imagination is liberated to express itself only when freedom has been ingrained within the performance instrument itself. Systematically dealing in advance with the technical components of an art, be it painting, dancing, sculpturing, building, composing, fiction writing, string playing, wind playing, keyboarding, or singing, franchises the artist to operate in a world of imagination and inspiration. Art and technique become wedded in a durable and productive relationship.

Appendix

Several Matters concerning Female Vocal Health

A MAIN PREMISE OF THIS BOOK HAS BEEN THAT EFFICIENT VOCALISM means healthy vocalism; a second tenet is the necessity for the daily routining of an effective technique; a third is physical health; and a fourth, vocal longevity. Because the vocal instrument is the whole body, not just the larynx, it is impossible to maintain healthy vocalism unless the body is well conditioned and continues to maintain that condition with the passing of time.

A prime consideration for the public performer is body weight. The ideal weight for singing is that which is ideal for the pursuit of any vital activity that involves energy and mobility. It is a mistake to assume that additional avoirdupois is advantageous to resonance. Placing a green felt protective pad around the pianoforte does not increase its "projection" or its resonance, nor do an extra twenty or thirty pounds increase a singer's vocal potency. Obesity produces short-winded singers, as is evidenced by the out-of-breath appearance of some well-known overweight performers at the conclusion of high-lying, sustained phrases.

In the current professional performance world the visual impact is as significant as the audible, and equally essential to career building. Young singers who aim for careers should not let the continued public success of a few overweight premier singers with remarkable voices mislead them into thinking that emerging singers may follow those models with impunity. Today's public wants the soprano who portrays a heroine of physical beauty to approach an ideal image. (Nor are the tenor and the baritone who portray the lover on today's stage exempt from corporeal demands. Obesity is an impediment to the career goal of any singer.)

What of the dramatic soprano? Do not the demands of her literature forego this physical expectation? Despite a few notable individual exceptions, the category of dramatic soprano must be included in this discussion regarding physical appearance. In any event, the number of females who potentially are vocally and technically appropriate to Turandot or to the Brünnhildes is exceedingly small. The dramatic soprano is not counted upon to be sylphlike, nor to present the appearance of her soubrette colleague. But her body proportions must not belie reasonable expectations of the dramatic situation. Unfortunately, a young overweight soprano may mistake her own weight condition as an appropriate qualification for meeting dramatic soprano demands and falsely attempt to adapt her vocalism to her physical state.

If a soprano who is serious about a career finds herself battling excess weight, she must avoid crash dieting. When one suddenly shuts down the level of nutritional intake, the body retains its calorie reservoir in order to preserve itself. Far better advice is to establish a program of gradual weight reduction by curtailment of foods that are high in fat and calories and initiating a daily exercise routine. Today's singer is surrounded by quantities of information on both topics; to ignore it may prove disastrous to career development. For the highly talented but overweight singer, professional assistance in bringing physical weight under control may be as vital as voice instruction and coaching.

The best diet for a singer is the best diet for living. To be avoided are foods that tend to induce gastric disturbance: deep-fried items, heavy and spicy sauces, and nearly all things on the fast-food menu. A major breakthrough for singers is the fuller realization within the medical community of the profound effect gastric reflux may have on the singing voice. Recent medications for reflux have become increasingly effective, and any singer who suffers from this malady should immediately seek medical advice. Slight elevation of the head of the bed and avoidance of dining or snacking near retiring are two practical means for helping to alleviate gastric reflux.

Any food or drink that acts as a desiccant should be avoided or its intake radically reduced, especially on performance days. This includes all alcoholic drinks, coffee, tea, colas, and foods with a high salt content (olives, potato chips, soups high in sodium, and many spices). The singer need not forgo the joys of eating, but she must judiciously restrict and balance foods and libations that may dry out the mucous membranes. If wine is a part of dining, the singer should drink a glass of water for any glass of wine imbibed. Hard liquors ought never to come into consideration for the dedicated singing artist. No singer should use any alcoholic beverage on a performance day.

There is now general awareness of the long-range dangers of tobacco use and of ambient tobacco smoke. What may not be as apparent are the immediate effects of smoking on the voice. Cigarette smoking produces thermotrauma, drying out the membrane of the vocal folds. A single cigarette will paralyze the cilia, the minuscule hairlike processes that line the nasal cavity, the trachea, and the bronchi, and which, by their constant propulsive action, assist in the removal of mucus and dust particles. No singer seriously considering a professional career can continue to smoke. Marijuana smoke has been reported to be four times as destructive to the vocal folds as tobacco smoke.

By now, most singers are aware of the desirability of avoiding medications that are desiccants. Clearly, certain physical conditions require medicines that have a drying effect; perhaps most common among the desiccants are the antihistamines.

When possible, aspirin—the oldest of the wonder drugs—should also be shunned by singers, because it may induce capillary fragility in certain vocal-fold conditions involving edema (slight swelling). Singers with serious physical problems ought to adopt, with their physician's advice, a plan for minimizing the desiccating aspects of medical treatment.

Dr. Van Lawrence, an esteemed otolaryngologist who examined and advised many professional singers, proposed a rubric that has found an endearing and permanent place in voice pedagogy: "Sing wet and pee pale." As a means for proper maintenance of body hydration levels, Lawrence recommended that a singer should periodically check that his or her urine remain "the color of tap water." Although Lawrence may have indulged in exaggeration to make his point, discolored urine is an indication that body tissues are not receiving appropriate hydration. This is of particular consequence for the laryngeal tissues. The suggestion to keep well hydrated does not mean carrying water onstage to sip between pieces, but routinely establishing the appropriate hydration level in the body far in advance of performance.

Singers need eight or more hours of sleep per night. Even the nonsinger will recognize a change in voice quality following a sleepless night. It is essential that today's young singers, both female and male, be made aware of the necessity for adequate sleep. Given the lifestyles on contemporary college and university campuses, getting adequate sleep becomes a major concern for the committed young singer and for her voice teacher.

Excessive talking can be disastrous to the singing voice, even if speech production is efficient. Speaking over ambient noise for an hour can be far more tiring than heavy singing for the same period of time. The noise levels of automobiles, buses, airplanes, discos, restaurants, parties, stadiums, and classrooms are potentially hazardous for a singer's vocal health.

At various points in this book, differences between male and female laryngeal structure have been mentioned, and the effects of puberty on the vocal instruments of the two genders have been discussed. Among adult vocalists, the most telling disadvantages for women are menstruation and the maturation and geriatric processes.

The effects of premenstrual syndrome (PMS) and menstrual periods on the voice need to be taken into account by every female singer. Some females experience a marked incidence of aches and pains or food cravings, and a great many suffer from water retention in the vocal folds during the premenstrual period. There is accumulating evidence that calcium deficiencies will exacerbate these conditions. Thomas H. Maugh, writing in the *Los Angeles Times*, quotes Michael A. Thomas, M.D., of the University of Cincinnati Medical Center:[1]

> Now, before I bring out the "big gun" treatments of prescription drug therapy, I will recommend to my patients they try calcium as a first-line therapy. . . . At best, they'll get relief from their PMS, and if not, they'll be getting a nutrient that their body needs to build strong bones.

A major drawback of PMS is that edema occurs during its period of influence. The body does not significantly differentiate among sphincters, and the larynx (which serves as a sphincter) undergoes swelling. Some female singers notice little change during the premenstrual period, but others find that pitches in the upper range are difficult to negotiate. For that reason, caution should be taken during the menstrual cycle with regard to vocalizing at the upper extremes of the voice. Whereas for the upper range the vocal folds should be tensing and elongating and their mass diminishing, edema associated with PMS makes the folds less supple.

With regard to hormonal alterations, although the male also experiences changes as the decades mount, it is the female who is most subject to their consequence. No teacher of singing, regardless of how much he or she is aware of problems caused by hormonal changes, ought to offer the female singer advice on this topic. Such a complex matter belongs in the hands of a physician, who should understand that his patient is a professional voice user.

The effects of the hormonal changes that are an inevitable part of the aging process are of concern to all adult female singers. Specialists at the Institute for Advanced Study of the Communication Processes, University of Florida, Gainesville, in an article on age-related voice measures among adult women, remark:[2]

> there are considerable reports in the geriatric literature that substantiate certain physiological changes that could disrupt the normal process of speech and voice production . . . reductions in vital capacity, osteoporosis of the rib and spinal column, ossification of the laryngeal cartilages, and atrophy as well as other age-related changes in respiratory, laryngeal, and facial musculature and mucosa.

In a discussion on vocal longevity and nutrition, Harvey and Miller suggest:[3]

> Generally, physiologic adaptations expected in aging include changes in cardiovascular characteristics, pulmonary function, hormonal balance, immune response, musculoskeletal integrity, and central nervous system function. Specific to laryngeal function, age-related degenerative changes include muscle atrophy, ligament deterioration, ossification of the . . . cartilages, slowing of neural transmission, and nerve conduction velocity.

The authors conclude:

> Informed nutrition—combined with exercise—can create an optimal environment for the long-term health that is essential to an enduring career in voice performance.

Most studies of the mature female voice have been directed toward the speaking voice, but because of the close relationship between the speaking and singing voices (being one instrument), research on the aging process in the spoken voice pertains to the singing voice as well. A cooperative study involving thirty-nine trained female singers and thirty-nine female nonsingers conducted by researchers from the University of Florida, Gainesville, the Cleveland Clinic Foundation, and a prominent New York City voice instructor, concluded that[4]

> the SFF [speaking fundamental frequency] and intensity levels were significantly higher for the professionals in comparison to the nonsingers, but only for certain age groups. Moreover, whereas the nonsinger SFF levels varied significantly as a function of age, those for the professional singers did not. . . . These results would reinforce the hypothesis . . . that sopranos may work to maintain their higher singing levels throughout life, and since they are adept at doing so, successfully resist the usual effects of advancing age and the expected lowering of the mean SFF.

Following a listing of deteriorating bodily functions associated with aging, other authors conclude:[5]

> The notion that this decline occurs gradually and progressively (linear senescence) is open to challenge. It appears possible that many of these functions can be maintained at a better level than expected until very near the end of life, perhaps allowing a high-quality singing or acting career to extend into or beyond the seventh decade.

These sources underscore the importance of the daily technique regimen advocated in this work. Dancer Martha Graham's longevity syndrome applies to the vocal art: never stop dancing (singing), and acquired disciplined mental and physical responses, although reduced, will continue their functions for you.

Notes

1. Categories of the Female Voice

1. Roger Parker, ed., *The Oxford Illustrated History of Opera* (Oxford: Oxford University Press, 1994), 56.

2. Parker, *Opera*, 68.

3. Parker, *Opera*, 51.

2. Registration Events in Female Voices

1. Ingo Titze, "Physiologic and Acoustic Differences between Male and Female Voices," *Journal of the Acoustical Society of America* 85, no. 4 (1980): 1699–1707.

2. Nellie Melba, *Melba Method* (London: Chappell, 1926).

4. Breath Energy in Singing

1. Donald Proctor, "Breath: The Power Source for the Voice," *NATS Journal* (Nov.–Dec. 1980): 26.

2. Ingo Titze, *Principles of Voice Production* (Englewood Cliffs, N.J.: Prentice-Hall, 1994), 62.

3. Proctor, "Breath," 26.

4. Harm K. Schutte and Richard Miller, *Breath Management in Repeated Vocal Onset* (Basle: Folia Phoniatrica, 1984), 225–32.

5. Francesco Lamperti, *Treatise on the Art of Singing* (London: G. Ricordi, [c. 1860]), 33.

6. Earl Brown, *Vocal Wisdom: Maxims of Giovanni Battista Lamperti* (New York: Hudson Offset), 1953.

6. Resonance in Soprano Voices

1. Thomas Baer et al., "Articulation and Voice Quality," in *Transcripts of the Seventh Symposium: Care of the Professional Voice*, part 1, ed. V. Lawrence (New York: Voice Foundation, 1972), 48–51.

2. Johan Sundberg, "The Voice as a Sound Generator," in *Research Aspects in Singing* (Stockholm: Royal Swedish Academy of Music, 1981), 6–14.

3. Richard Miller, *The Structure of Singing* (New York: Schirmer, 1986), 298.

4. Ibid., p. 299

5. Richard Miller, "The Solo Singer in the Choral Ensemble," in *Choral Journal* 35, no. 8 (1995): 31–36.

7. Nasal Continuants as Assists in Resonance Balancing

1. Michael Benninger et al., "Flexible Direct Nasopharyngolaryngoscopy in Association with Vocal Pedagogy," in *Medical Problems of Performing Artists* (Denver: 1989), 163–167.

2. See, e.g., Thomas Fillebrown, *Resonance in Singing and Speaking* (Bryn Mawr: Oliver Ditson, 1911); Wilbur Bartholomew, *Acoustics of Music* (New York: Prentice-Hall, 1942); Peter Ladefoged, *Elements of Acoustics* (Chicago: University of Chicago Press, 1962), 105; Ralph Appelman, *The Science of Vocal Pedagogy* (Bloomington: Indiana University Press, 1967), 73–78; William Vennard, *Singing: The Mechanism and the Technic* (New York: Carl Fischer, 1967), 93–96; Gunnar Fant, "Phonetics and Speech Research," in *Research Potentials in Voice Physiology*, ed. David Brewer (Syracuse: State University of New York, 1964), 230–233; Fred Minifie, "Speech Acoustics," in *Normal Aspects of Speech, Hearing, and Language*, ed. Fred Minifie, Thomas Hixon, and Frederick Williams (Englewood Cliffs, N.J.: Prentice-Hall 1973), 235–284; Ingo Titze, "Nasality in Vowels," *NATS Journal* 43, no. 4 (1987): 34; Michael Benninger et al., "Flexible Direct Nasoopharyngolaryngoscopy," 163–167; and William McIver and Richard Miller, "A Brief Study of Nasality in Singing," *Journal of Singing* (Mar.–Apr. 1996): 21–26.

10. Soprano Vocal Registration and Vowel Modification (Aggiustamento)

1. William Vennard, *Singing: The Mechanism and the Technic* (New York: Carl Fisher, 1967), 54–55.

2. Manuel Garcia, *Hints on Singing* (London: Ascherberg, Hopwood, and Crew, 1894).

3. Richard Miller, *The Structure of Singing* (New York: Schirmer, 1986), 196.

4. Ingo Titze, *Principles of Voice Production* (Englewood Cliffs, N.J.: Prentice-Hall, 1994), 293.

Appendix

1. Thomas H. Maugh II, "Calcium Cuts Symptoms of PMS by Half, Study Shows," *Los Angeles Times*, 24 Aug. 1998.

2. Richard Morris and W. S. Brown, "Age-Related Voice Measures among Adult Women," *Journal of Voice* 1, no. 1 (1987): 38.

3. Pamela Harvey and Susan Miller, "Nutrition and the Professional Voice User," in *Vocal Health and Pedagogy*, ed. Robert Sataloff (San Diego: Singular Publishing Group, 1998), 210–211.

4. W. S. Brown Jr. et al., "Phonational Profiles of Female Professional Singers and Non-singers," *Journal of Voice* 7, no. 3, (1973): 220.

5. Robert Sataloff, Joseph Spiegel, and Deborah Caputo Rosen, "The Effects of Age on the Voice," in *Vocal Health and Pedagogy*, ed. Robert Sataloff (San Diego: Singular Publishing Group, 1998), 128.

Index